Heike Jauernig/Jasmin Boller

Englisch an Stationen

Handlungsorientierte Materialien zu den Kernthemen der

Klasse 3

Druck und Bindung: Korrekt Nyomdaipari Kft., Budapest

Auer

Die Herausgeber:

Marco Bettner – Rektor als Ausbildungsleiter, Haupt- und Realschullehrer,
Referent in der Lehrerfort- und Lehrerweiterbildung,
zahlreiche Veröffentlichungen als Autor und Herausgeber

Dr. Erik Dinges – Rektor einer Förderschule für Lernhilfe,
Referent in der Lehrerfort- und Lehrerweiterbildung,
zahlreiche Veröffentlichungen als Autor und Herausgeber

Die Autorinnen:

Heike Jauernig – Fremdsprachenlehrerin an einer internationalen Schule und Autorin
Jasmin Boller – Grundschullehrerin und Autorin

6. Auflage 2020
© Auer Verlag
AAP Lehrerwelt GmbH, Augsburg
Alle Rechte vorbehalten
Illustrationen: Corina Beurenmeister
Satz: Fotosatz H. Buck, Kumhausen
Druck und Bindung: Korrekt Nyomdaipari Kft., Budapest
ISBN 978-3-403-06149-6

www.auer-verlag.de

Inhalt

Vorwort 4

Lehrerinformationen 5

Materialaufstellung 6

Einzuführender Wortschatz 8

Colours and numbers

Station 1:   Let's count! 10
Station 2:   Telephone numbers 11
Station 3:   Read and colour! 12
Station 4:   My interview 13
Station 5:   Which colour is missing? 14
Station 6:   Which number is missing? 15
Station 7:   Colour the clown! 17
Station 8:   Let's go fishing! 18
Station 9:   My caterpillar 19

Christmas

Station 1:   What's missing? 20
Station 2:   Labels 21
Station 3:   Missing letters 22
Station 4:   Unscramble letters! 23
Station 5:   Colourful Christmas 24
Station 6:   Christmas in the USA 25
Station 7:   Christmas card 26

Pets

Station 1:   Mime! 27
Station 2:   Pictionary 28
Station 3:   Profile 29
Station 4:   Happy families 30
Station 5:   Read and write! 33
Station 6:   Word search puzzle 34
Station 7:   Odd one out! 35

Clothes

Station 1:   Odd one out! 36
Station 2:   Who is it? 37

Station 3:   Read and draw! 38
Station 4:   Listen and draw! 39
Station 5:   Happy families 40
Station 6:   Cross word puzzle 43
Station 7:   Labels 44

Hobbies

Station 1:   Mime! 45
Station 2:   Missing letters 46
Station 3:   My interview 47
Station 4:   Listen and draw! 48
Station 5:   Who is it? 49
Station 6:   Labels 50
Station 7:   Creative writing 51

Food

Fruit
Station 1:   Happy families 52
Station 2:   My interview 55
Station 3:   Colourful fruit 56
Station 4:   Word search puzzle 57

Breakfast
Station 5:   Having breakfast 58
Station 6:   Word shapes 59
Station 7:   Read and draw! 60
Station 8:   My interview 61
Station 9:   Odd one out! 62
Station 10: Unscramble letters! 63

Sandwiches
Station 11: Sandwiches 64
Station 12: Cross word puzzle 65
Station 13: Missing letters 66
Station 14: Odd one out! 67
Station 15: Unscramble letters! 68

Anhang

Laufzettel 69
Lösungen 70

Vorwort

Bei den vorliegenden Stationsarbeiten handelt es sich um eine Arbeitsform, bei der unterschiedliche Lernvoraussetzungen, unterschiedliche Zugänge und Betrachtungsweisen und unterschiedliche Lern- und Arbeitstempi der Schülerinnen und Schüler Berücksichtigung finden. Die Grundidee ist, den Schülerinnen und Schülern einzelne Arbeitsstationen anzubieten, an denen sie gleichzeitig selbstständig arbeiten können. Die Reihenfolge des Bearbeitens der einzelnen Stationen ist dabei ebenso frei wählbar wie das Arbeitstempo und meist auch die Sozialform.

Als dominierende Unterrichtsprinzipien sind bei allen Stationen die Schülerorientierung und Handlungsorientierung aufzuführen. Schülerorientierung meint, dass der Lehrer in den Hintergrund tritt und nicht mehr im Mittelpunkt der Interaktion steht. Er wird zum Beobachter, Berater und Moderator. Seine Aufgabe ist nicht das Strukturieren und Darbieten des Lerngegenstandes in kleinsten Schritten, sondern durch die vorbereiteten Stationen eine Lernatmosphäre zu schaffen, in der Schülerinnen und Schüler sich Unterrichtsinhalte eigenständig erarbeiten bzw. Lerninhalte festigen und vertiefen können. Handlungsorientierung meint, dass das angebotene Material und die Arbeitsaufträge für sich selbst sprechen. Der Unterrichtsgegenstand und die zu gewinnenden Erkenntnisse werden nicht durch den Lehrer dargeboten, sondern durch die Auseinandersetzung mit dem Material und die eigene Tätigkeit gewonnen und begriffen.

Ziel der Veröffentlichung ist, wie oben angesprochen, das Anknüpfen an unterschiedliche Lernvoraussetzungen der Schülerinnen und Schüler. Jeder Einzelne erhält seinen eigenen Zugang zum inhaltlichen Lernstoff. Die einzelnen Stationen ermöglichen das Lernen mit allen Sinnen bzw. den verschiedenen Eingangskanälen. Dabei werden sowohl visuelle (sehorientierte) als auch haptische (fühlorientierte) und auch intellektuelle Lerntypen angesprochen. An dieser Stelle werden auch gleichermaßen die Bruner'schen Repräsentationsebenen (enaktiv bzw. handelnd, ikonisch bzw. visuell und symbolisch) mit einbezogen. Aus Ergebnissen der Wissenschaft ist bekannt: Je mehr Eingangskanäle angesprochen werden, umso besser und langfristiger wird Wissen gespeichert und damit umso fester verankert. Das vorliegende Arbeitsheft unterstützt in diesem Zusammenhang das Erinnerungsvermögen, das nicht nur an Einzelheiten und Begriffen geknüpft ist, sondern häufig auch an die Lernstation.

Folgende Inhalte des Englischunterrichts werden innerhalb der verschiedenen Stationen behandelt:

- colours and numbers
- Christmas
- pets
- clothes
- hobbies
- food

Lehrerinformationen

Im Fremdsprachenunterricht der Grundschule sollen neben den beiden Fertigkeiten Hören und Sprechen auch Lesen und Schreiben phasenweise im Rahmen einer Unterrichtseinheit angeboten werden, **nachdem** der neue Wortschatz phonetisch gesichert wurde.

Das Schreiben der aus mündlichen Anwendungen und durch Leseaufgaben vertrauten Wörter hat dabei eine lernunterstützende Funktion. Gemäß Lehrplan schreiben Kinder Wörter nach Vorlage ab und fügen sie beispielsweise in Lückentexte ein.

Aus lernpsychologischer Sicht ist es für das dauerhafte Memorieren günstiger, wenn ein neu zu erlernendes Wort nicht nur als akustischer Reiz, sondern möglichst in einer Kombination mit anderen Sinnesreizen, wie etwa durch die gleichzeitige visuelle oder kinästhetische Unterstützung anhand des Schriftbildes oder des Schreibens, angeboten wird. So wirkt die Feinmotorik beim Abschreiben einzelner Wörter positiv auf die Einprägung.

Die Kopiervorlagen sind so gestaltet, dass durch Text und Bilder eine Differenzierung möglich ist. Leistungsschwächere Kinder können durch die Bilder den bereits eingeführten Wortschatz abrufen. Leistungsstarke Schülerinnen und Schüler hingegen können sich ausschließlich auf den Text konzentrieren.

Um das Prinzip der Einsprachigkeit im Englischunterricht der Grundschule gewährleisten zu können, wurden die Arbeitsanweisungen ausschließlich in Englisch verfasst und durch grafische Darstellungen unterstützt.

Die abwechslungsreichen Übungsformen dieser Stationsarbeiten eignen sich auch für Freiarbeitsphasen des täglichen Unterrichts.

Erklärung der Piktogramme

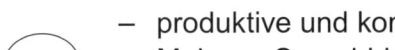

- produktive und kommunikative Sprachübung
- Mehrere Sprechblasen weisen auf Partner- bzw. Gruppenarbeit hin.
- Wird abwechselnd geübt, können Häkchen in die Sprechblasen am Ende des Arbeitsauftrages eingetragen werden.

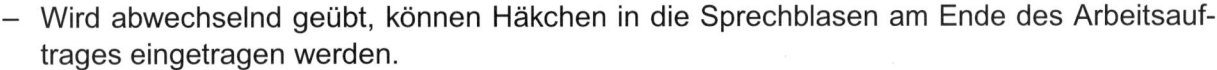

Schreibübung

Leseverständnis

ausmalen

Materialaufstellung

Colours and numbers

Station 1: Let's count!
- Arbeitsanweisung laminieren
- Streichhölzer
- Folienstift

Station 2: Telephone numbers
- 1 Klassensatz Kopien

Station 3: Read and colour!
- 1 Klassensatz Kopien

Station 4: My interview
- 1 Klassensatz Kopien

Station 5: Which colour is missing?
- Arbeitsanweisung laminieren
- Herzen in allen Farben anmalen, laminieren, ausschneiden
- Folienstift

Station 6: Which number is missing?
- Arbeitsanweisung laminieren
- Zahlen laminieren, ausschneiden
- Folienstift

Station 7: Colour the clown!
- 1 Klassensatz Kopien

Station 8: Let's go fishing!
- 1 Klassensatz Kopien
- Magnetangeln
- Büroklammern

Station 9: My caterpillar
- 1 Klassensatz Kopien

Christmas

Station 1: What's missing?
- Arbeitsanweisung laminieren
- Bilder anmalen, laminieren, ausschneiden
- Folienstift

Station 2: Labels
- 1 Klassensatz Kopien

Station 3: Missing letters
- 1 Klassensatz Kopien

Station 4: Unscramble letters!
- 1 Klassensatz Kopien

Station 5: Colourful Christmas
- 1 Klassensatz Kopien

Station 6: Christmas in the USA
- 1 Klassensatz Kopien

Station 7: Christmas card
- Arbeitsanweisung laminieren
- Tonpapier
- Folie
- Stifte bereitstellen

Pets

Station 1: Mime!
- Arbeitsanweisung laminieren
- Folienstift

Station 2: Pictionary
- 1 Klassensatz Kopien

Station 3: Profile
- 1 Klassensatz Kopien

Station 4: Happy families
- Quartett ca. 6- bis 7-mal kopieren, laminieren, ausschneiden

Station 5: Read and write!
- 1 Klassensatz Kopien

Station 6: Word search puzzle
- 1 Klassensatz Kopien

Station 7: Odd one out!
- 1 Klassensatz Kopien

Clothes

Station 1: Odd one out!
- 1 Klassensatz Kopien

Station 2: Who is it?
- Arbeitsanweisung laminieren
- Folienstift

Station 3: Read and draw!
- 1 Klassensatz Kopien

Station 4: Listen and draw!
- 1 Klassensatz Kopien

Station 5: Happy families
- Quartett ca. 6- bis 7-mal kopieren, laminieren, ausschneiden

Station 6: Cross word puzzle
- 1 Klassensatz Kopien

Station 7: Labels
- 1 Klassensatz Kopien

Hobbies

Station 1: Mime!
- Arbeitsanweisung laminieren
- Folienstift

Station 2: Missing letters
- 1 Klassensatz Kopien

Station 3: My interview
- 1 Klassensatz Kopien

Station 4: Listen and draw!
- 1 Klassensatz Kopien

Station 5: Who is it?
- 1 Klassensatz Kopien

Station 6: Labels
- 1 Klassensatz Kopien

Station 7: Creative writing
- 1 Klassensatz Kopien

Food

Fruit

Station 1: Happy families
- Quartett ca. 6- bis 7-mal kopieren, laminieren, ausschneiden

Station 2: My interview
- 1 Klassensatz Kopien

Station 3: Colourful fruit
- 1 Klassensatz Kopien

Station 4: Word search puzzle
- 1 Klassensatz Kopien

Breakfast

Station 5: Having breakfast
- 1 Klassensatz Kopien

Station 6: Word shapes
- 1 Klassensatz Kopien

Station 7: Read and draw!
- 1 Klassensatz Kopien

Station 8: My interview
- 1 Klassensatz Kopien

Station 9: Odd one out!
- 1 Klassensatz Kopien

Station 10: Unscramble letters!
- 1 Klassensatz Kopien

Sandwiches

Station 11: Sandwiches
- 1 Klassensatz Kopien

Station 12: Cross word puzzle
- 1 Klassensatz Kopien

Station 13: Missing letters
- 1 Klassensatz Kopien

Station 14: Odd one out!
- 1 Klassensatz Kopien

Station 15: Unscramble letters!
- 1 Klassensatz Kopien

Einzuführender Wortschatz

Colours and numbers

Vokabular: Zahlen von 1–20
red, green, yellow, blue, brown, white, black, orange, pink, purple, grey (dark/light)

Strukturen:
- Count!
- What's your telephone number? My telephone number is …
- What's your favourite number? My favourite number is …
- What's your favourite colour? My favourite colour is …
- Which number is missing? Three is missing.
- Which colour is missing? Red is missing.
- What colour is your …? My … is … (green).
- What colour is it? It's green.

Christmas

Vokabular: Santa Claus, reindeer, chimney, present, fireplace, sleigh, Christmas tree, stocking

Strukturen:
- What's missing? The … is missing.
- Dear …! Merry Christmas and a Happy New Year! With love, your …

Station 6 sollte als Storytelling vorgetragen werden, die Kinder müssen diese Strukturen nicht sprechen, aber verstehen können.

Wiederholung der Strukturen:
- What colour is your …? My … is …

Pets

Vokabular: dog, cat, rat, guinea pig, budgie, turtle, fish, rabbit

Strukturen:
- Are you a …? Yes, I am./No, I am not.
- Is it a …? Yes, it is./No it isn't.
- Have you got …? Yes, I have./No, I haven't.
- My pet's name is …
- My pet/It is … years/months old.
- My pet likes …
- My pet/It can …
- My pet lives in …
- My pet/It has got …

Wiederholung der Strukturen:
- What's your favourite pet? My favourite pet is a …
- What colour is your pet? My pet's colour is …

Clothes

Vokabular: t-shirt, blouse, shorts, jeans, pullover, jacket, coat, skirt, shirt, trousers, tights, socks, cap, hat, sweater, trainers, boots, shoes

Strukturen:
– The boy/girl/He/She is wearing …
– Who is it?

Wiederholung der Strukturen:
– Have you got …?   Yes, I have./No, I haven't.
– Is it …?   Yes, it is./No it isn't.

Hobbies

Vokabular: singing, reading, skiing, riding a horse, riding a bike, playing football, tennis, the piano, dancing, swimming

Strukturen:
– Do you like … ?   Yes, I do./No, I don't.
– I like …/I don't like …

Wiederholung der Strukturen:
– Are you …?   Yes, I am./No, I am not.
– Her/His name is …
– He/She has got …
– Her/His favourite pet/hobbies is/are a …
– Her/His favourite colour is …
– She/He is wearing …
– Her/His telephone number is …

Food

Vokabular: fruit: apple/s, cherr-y/ies, orange/s, pear/s, peach/es, strawberr-y/ies, banana/s, lemon/s
breakfast: butter, bread, eggs, milk, cheese, jam, honey, toast, hot chocolate
sandwich: lettuce, cucumbers, ham, salami, tomatoes, toast, bread, eggs, cheese

Strukturen:
– Can I have some … please?
– Here you are.
– Thank you.
– You're welcome.
– What do you like for breakfast?   I like …
– It's a sandwich with …

Wiederholung der Strukturen:
– Have you got …?   Yes, I have./No, I haven't.
– Do you like …?   Yes, I do./No, I don't.
– What colour is your …?   My … is …
– She/He likes …
– She/He has got a sandwich with …

1. Work with a partner  .

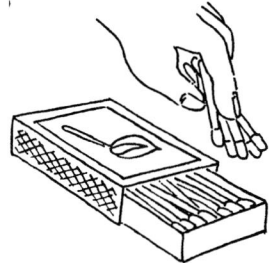

Put matches on the table.

 : "Count!"

 : "One, two, three …"

2. Take turns and tick ✓:

Heike Jauernig/Jasmin Boller: Englisch an Stationen (Klasse 3)
© Auer Verlag

 What's your telephone number?

 My telephone number is …

name	telephone number

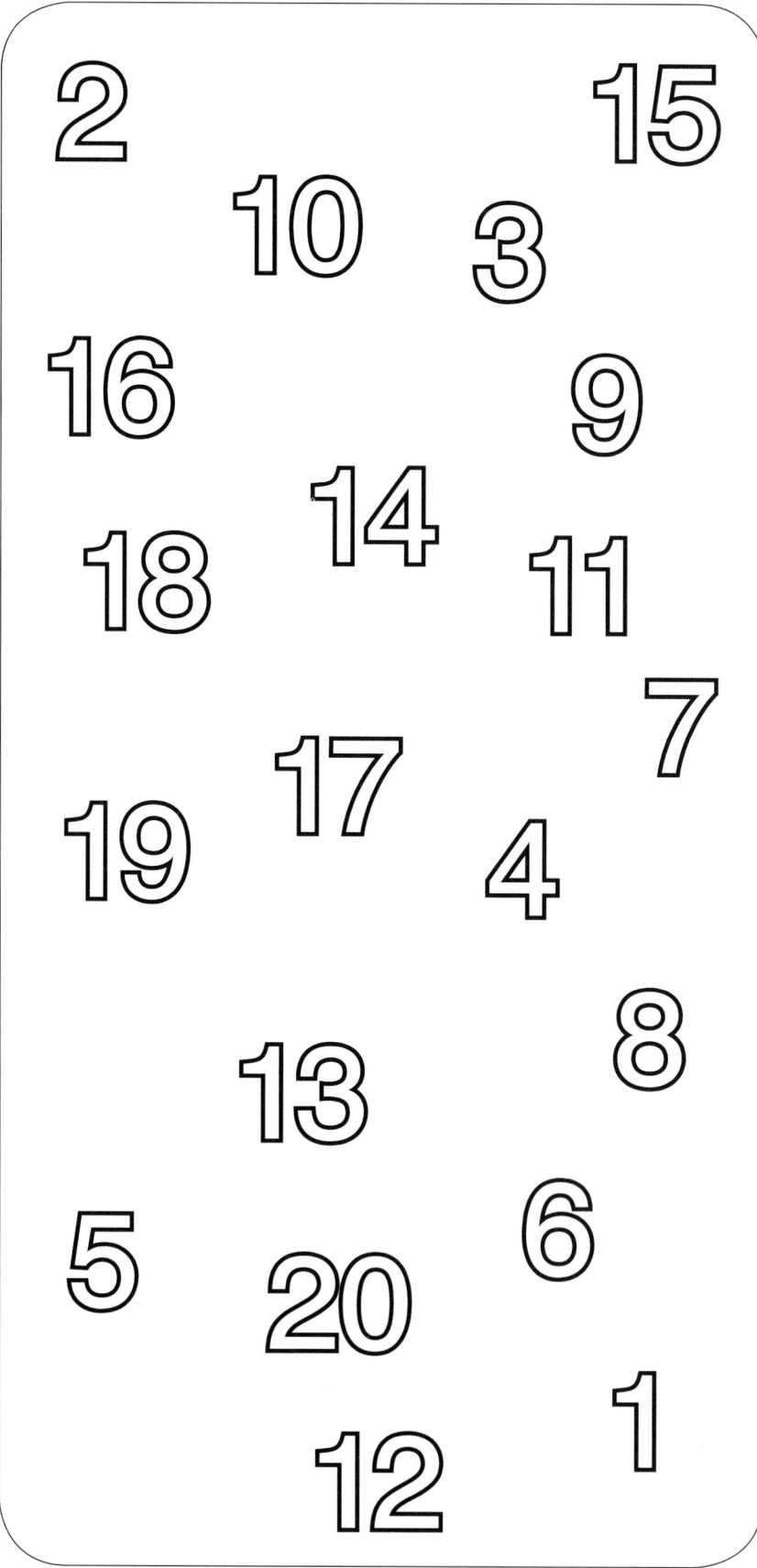
Read 👓 and colour ✏.

Seven is green.

Two is yellow.

Fifteen is purple.

Nine is grey.

Twenty is orange.

Fourteen is black.

Eleven is brown.

Three is white.

Eighteen is red.

Sixteen is dark blue.

Ten is pink.

One is red.

Four is light blue.

Five is dark green.

Six is purple.

Eight is light brown.

Twelve is black.

Thirteen is green.

Nineteen is blue.

Seventeen is pink.

2 15 10 3 16 9 14 18 11 7 19 17 4 13 8 5 20 6 1 12

Heike Jouernig/Jasmin Boller: Englisch an Stationen (Klasse 3)
© Auer Verlag

 What's your favourite colour?
What's your favourite number?

 My favourite colour is …
My favourite number is …

name	favourite colour	favourite number

Heike Jouernig/Jasmin Boller: Englisch an Stationen (Klasse 3)
© Auer Verlag

1. Work with a partner  .

 : "Close your eyes!"

Remove one card.

 : "Open your eyes! Which colour is missing?"

 : "(Red, blue …) is missing."

2. Take turns and tick ✓ :

Heike Jauernig/Jasmin Boller: Englisch an Stationen (Klasse 3)
© Auer Verlag

1. Work with a partner  .

 : "Close your eyes!"

Remove one card.

 : "Open your eyes! Which number is missing?"

 : "(Nine, six …) is missing."

2. Take turns and tick ✓: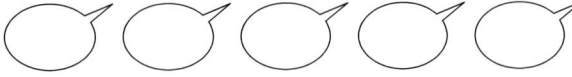

Die Herzen in den Farben weiß, gelb, orange, rosa, rot, lila, blau, grün, grau, braun und schwarz ausmalen.
Danach ausschneiden.

1	2	3	4
5	6	7	8
9	10	11	12
13	14	15	16
17	18	19	20

Heike Jauernig/Jasmin Boller: Englisch an Stationen (Klasse 3)
© Auer Verlag

Colour ✏.

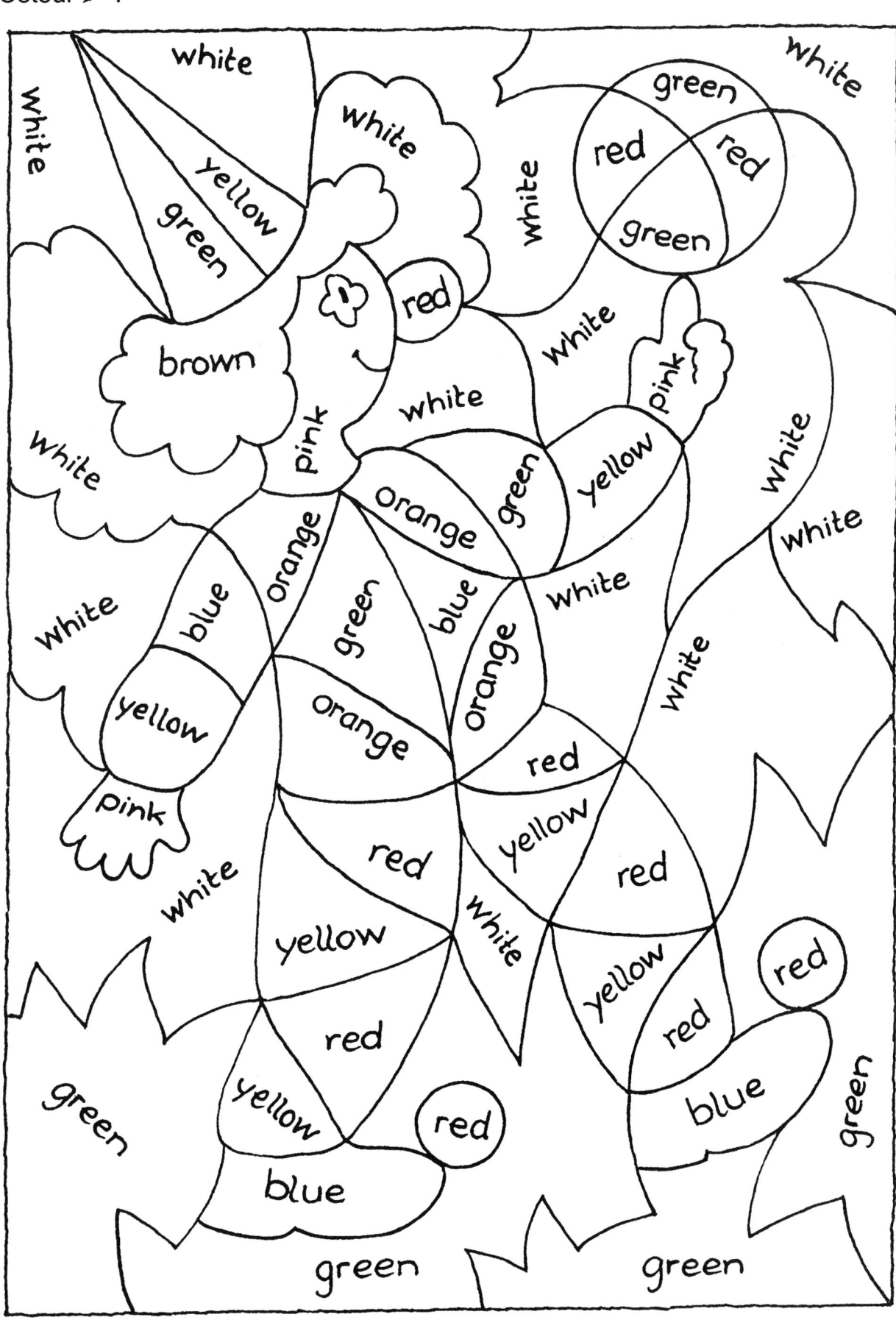

1. Colour  the fish and cut ✂ them out.

   Put paper clips ⟨⟩ on the fish.

2. Work with a partner . Go fishing .

 : "My fish is … (green, red, yellow …).
What colour is your fish?"

"My fish is …
What colour is your fish?"

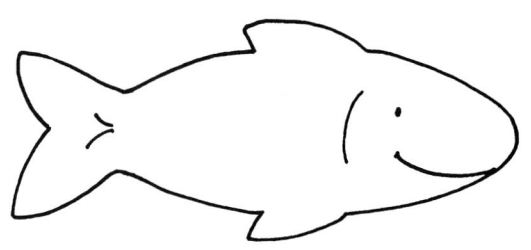
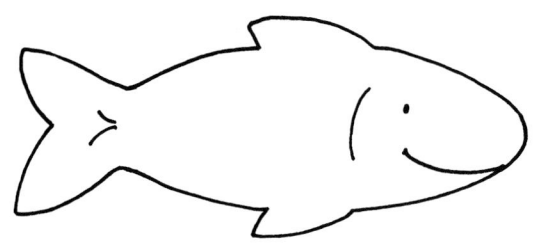

1. Colour  the .

> yellow   green   red   blue
> orange   white   brown   pink
> purple   black   grey

2. Work with a partner .

Point  to a colour and ask 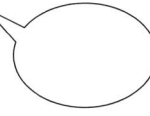 : "What colour is it?"

 : "It's … (blue, green, yellow …)."

3. Cut out ✂ the words and glue 🖌 them next to the correct colour.

white	yellow	orange	red	pink	blue
purple	green	brown	grey	black	

 Write ✏ the words next to the correct colour.

1.  Work with a partner 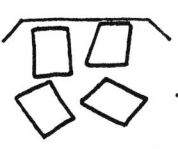 .

 : "Close your eyes!"

"Remove one card."

 : "Open your eyes. What's missing?"

 : "The … (present, stocking …) is missing."

2. Take turns and tick ✓ :

Heike Jauernig/Jasmin Boller: Englisch an Stationen (Klasse 3)
© Auer Verlag

Fill in ✎.

present   Santa Claus   reindeer   chimney

fireplace   sleigh   Christmas tree   stocking

Fill in the missing letters ____✎.

___ein ___eer

___rese___t

Ch___ist___a___ ___ree

___ire___lace

s___eigh

S___nt___ Clau___

ch___m___ey

s___ock___ng

s i n a r m
t f l n p a
t s p d i r

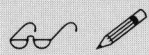
Unscramble the letters and write _____ ✏ the words.

y
e n m
i ch

_____

l a
a u a
s S n
C t

_____

i e l
s gh

_____

t s
e r p
e n

_____

e n
e r e
r i d

_____

ck o
g n
i t s

_____

s a
m s t
i r e Ch
e r t

_____

e a
p l e r
i f c

_____

1. Colour  the pictures.

2. Work with a partner .

 : "My … (stocking …) is … (green, red, yellow …).
What colour is your … (stocking)?"

: "My … (stocking …) is …
What colour is your … (sleigh …)?"

  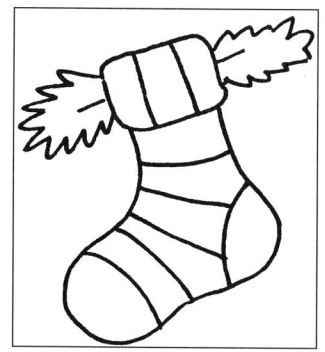 

Cut out ✂ the sentences. Glue the sentences under the correct picture.

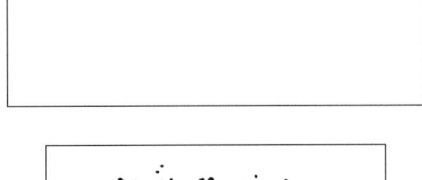  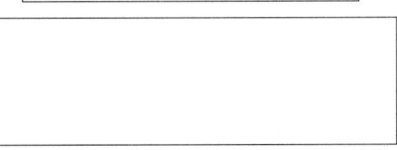

 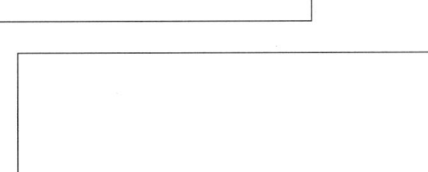 

Santa Claus comes at night.	He has got a sleigh.	He puts the big presents under the Christmas tree.
The reindeer pull the sleigh.	Santa Claus comes down the chimney.	On December 25 in the morning, the children look inside the stockings.
The children put stockings on the fire-place on Christmas Eve.	He puts the presents into the stockings.	

Heike Jouernig/Jasmin Boller: Englisch an Stationen (Klasse 3)
© Auer Verlag

Making a Christmas card

1. Draw  a Christmas picture on white paper 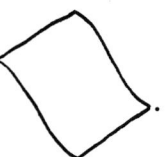 .

2. Glue  the picture on red or green cardboard  .

3. Write  :

> Dear … (Mom, Dad, Jane, Ben …)!
>
> Merry Christmas and
> a Happy New Year!
>
> With love, your … (your name)

4. Decorate your Christmas card.

     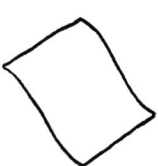

Heike Jauernig/Jasmin Boller: Englisch an Stationen (Klasse 3)
© Auer Verlag

1. Work with a partner  .

2. Mime a pet (dog, cat, budgie …).

: "Are you a …?"

"Yes, I am."/"No, I am not."

3. Take turns and tick ✓ :

1. Work with a partner  .

2. Draw ✏ a pet (turtle, guinea pig, rat …).

"Is it a …?"

:   "Yes, it is."/"No, it isn't."

3. Take turns.

Heike Jouernig/Jasmin Boller: Englisch an Stationen (Klasse 3)
© Auer Verlag

Fill out ____✏.

Present it in class.

My favourite pet is a _____.

My pet's colour is _____.

My pet's name is _____.

Draw ✏ your pet.

My pet is ☐ one year old.

☐ ____ years old.

☐ one month old.

☐ ____ months old.

My pet likes ☐ carrots.

☐ insects.

☐ seeds.

☐ meat.

My pet has got ☐ two legs.

☐ four legs.

☐ a tail.

☐ wings.

My pet can ☐ swim.

☐ fly.

☐ run.

☐ jump.

My pet lives in ☐ a cage.

☐ a tank.

☐ the house.

☐ the garden.

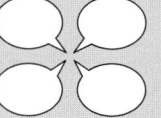
1. Work with partners

2. Hand out all the cards to the players .

 : "Have you got … (2 dogs, 4 cats …)?"

 : "Yes, I have. Here you are."
"No, I haven't."

3. Take turns.

16	17	18

15

fifteen fish

15	17	18

16

sixteen fish

15	16	18

17

seventeen fish

15	16	17

18

eighteen fish

18	19	20

17

seventeen turtles

17	19	20

18

eighteen turtles

17	18	20

19

nineteen turtles

17	18	19

20

twenty turtles

3	4	5

2

two guinea pigs

2	4	5

3

three guinea pigs

2	3	5

4

four guinea pigs

2	3	4

5

five guinea pigs

7	8	9

6

six budgies

6	8	9

7

seven budgies

6	7	9

8

eight budgies

6	7	8

9

nine budgies

Heike Jouernig/Jasmin Boller: Englisch an Stationen (Klasse 3)
© Auer Verlag

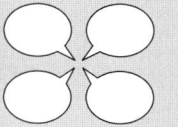

10	11	12

9

nine rats

9	11	12

10
ten rats

9	10	12

11
eleven rats

9	10	11

12
twelve rats

11	12	13

10
ten dogs

10	12	13

11
eleven dogs

10	11	13

12
twelve dogs

10	11	12

13
thirteen dogs

13	14	15

12
twelve cats

12	14	15

13
thirteen cats

12	13	15

14
fourteen cats

12	13	14

15
fifteen cats

14	15	16

13
thirteen rabbits

13	15	16

14
fourteen rabbits

13	14	16

15
fifteen rabbits

13	14	15

16
sixteen rabbits

Heike Jauernig/Jasmin Boller: Englisch an Stationen (Klasse 3)
© Auer Verlag

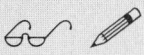
Fill in the correct words.

This is a _____ .

It can _____ .

This is a _____ .

Its colour is _____ .

Amy has got a _____ .

It is _____ years old.

This is a _____ .

It can _____ .

This is Bryan's _____ .

It has got two _____ .

Jillian has got a _____ .

Its colour is _____ .

This is Matt's _____ .

It has got four _____ .

Kate has got a _____ .

Its colour is _____ .

| budgie |
| turtle |
| rat |
| fish |
| guinea pig |
| dog |
| rabbit |
| cat |
| swim |
| run |
| legs |
| eyes |
| six |
| brown |
| white |
| black |

Heike Jauernig/Jasmin Boller: Englisch an Stationen (Klasse 3)
© Auer Verlag

C	V	Z	X	C	M	T	B	U	D	G	I	E	R	N
F	B	T	Y	P	E	L	J	X	Y	O	D	A	T	N
A	K	I	U	C	S	T	U	R	T	L	E	Z	U	F
M	J	D	T	P	H	K	W	P	K	G	Q	R	G	T
N	R	X	U	I	D	Y	T	W	Q	S	L	A	I	U
X	R	K	Z	M	J	G	X	C	S	H	V	T	S	C
T	A	Q	L	A	M	R	J	C	Q	J	I	D	O	G
W	B	X	O	F	D	J	F	A	O	Z	P	A	H	K
F	B	U	G	P	R	M	E	T	L	D	F	A	T	V
Q	I	J	G	U	I	N	E	A	X	P	I	G	E	H
X	T	M	D	J	Z	G	H	W	K	O	S	F	X	E
P	R	Z	A	W	Z	V	K	I	H	N	H	X	U	S
Q	E	S	F	Y	G	A	B	R	P	G	B	Y	I	X
E	R	R	M	F	G	V	Y	M	O	B	Q	F	M	U
I	I	A	Z	U	O	N	N	W	Z	O	N	C	Z	Z

CAT

DOG

BUDGIE

RABBIT

GUINEA PIG

FISH

RAT

TURTLE

Colour the word and the picture in the same colour.

green

blue

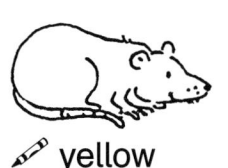
yellow

purple

orange

red

pink

red

grey

Heike Jauernig/Jasmin Boller: Englisch an Stationen (Klasse 3)
© Auer Verlag

Cross out ✕ ✎ the pet that is different.

These pets can run:

These pets have got four legs:

These pets cannot climb:

These pets have got ears:

These pets cannot fly:

Heike Jouernig/Jasmin Boller: Englisch an Stationen (Klasse 3)
© Auer Verlag

Cross the odd one out ✕ ✏ .   Why is it different _____ ✏ ?

1.	t-shirt	blouse	~~nine~~	shorts	number
2.	trainers	budgie	boots	shoes	_____
3.	hair	jeans	pullover	shorts	_____
4.	jacket	coat	green	blouse	_____
5.	skirt	seven	shirt	trousers	_____
6.	tights	dress	skirt	dog	_____
7.	turtle	socks	cap	hat	_____
8.	sweater	trainers	coat	purple	_____
9.	foot	shirt	jacket	shoes	_____
10.	t-shirt	white	tights	jeans	_____

t-shirt   blouse   shorts   jeans   pullover   jacket

coat   skirt   shirt   trousers   tights   socks

cap   hat   sweater   trainers   boots   shoes

1. Work with a partner .

2. Describe a boy/a girl in your class:

 : "The boy is wearing … (a blue t-shirt, black trousers …). Who is it?"

 : "Is it … (Kevin, Jack …)?"

 : "Yes, it is."/"No, it isn't."

3. Take turns and tick ✓ :

Read 🕮 and draw 🖊 the clothes.

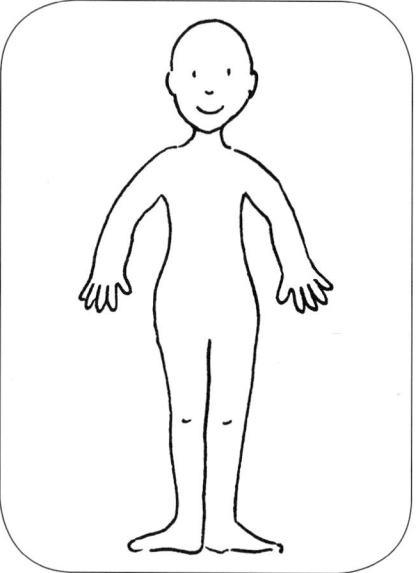

The girl is wearing a red and yellow dress. She is wearing grey shoes. Her hair is black.

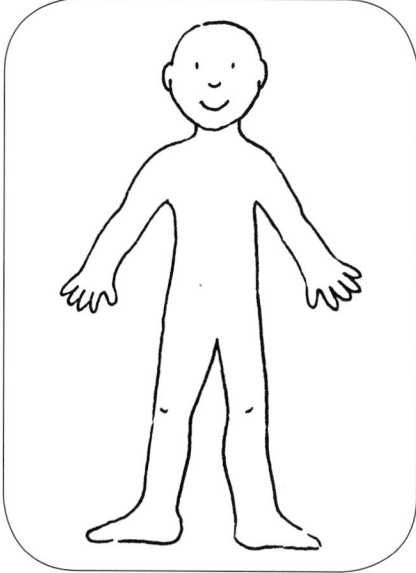

The boy is wearing a green sweater, brown trousers and black shoes. His hair is brown. A blue jacket is in his hand.

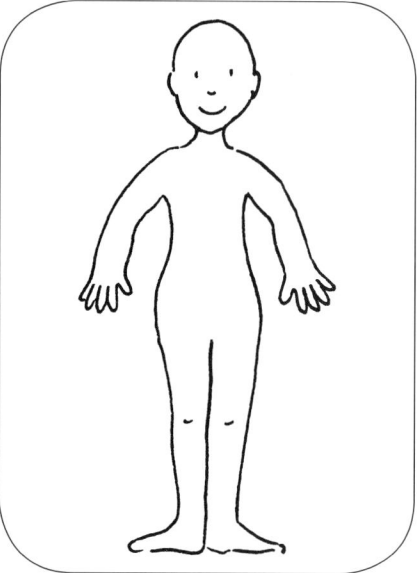

This girl is wearing a pink blouse, a blue skirt, purple socks and green shoes. Her hair is dark brown.

This boy is wearing orange jeans and a black and green t-shirt. His trainers are green, too. His hair is blonde.

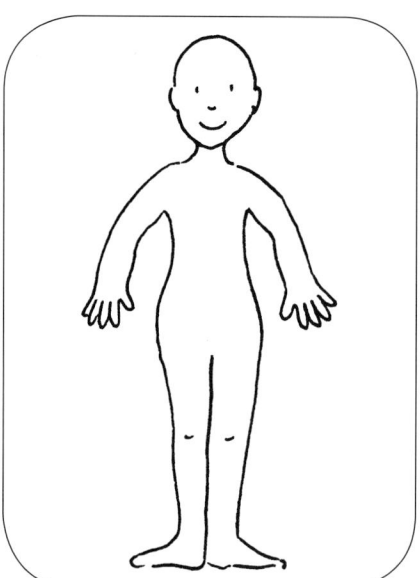

The girl is wearing a red coat and a white hat. Her tights are blue and her boots are grey. Her hair is blonde, too.

The boy is wearing a blue shirt, black shorts and a yellow cap. His trainers are white. His hair is red.

Heike Jauernig/Jasmin Boller: Englisch an Stationen (Klasse 3)
© Auer Verlag

1. Work with a partner  .

2. 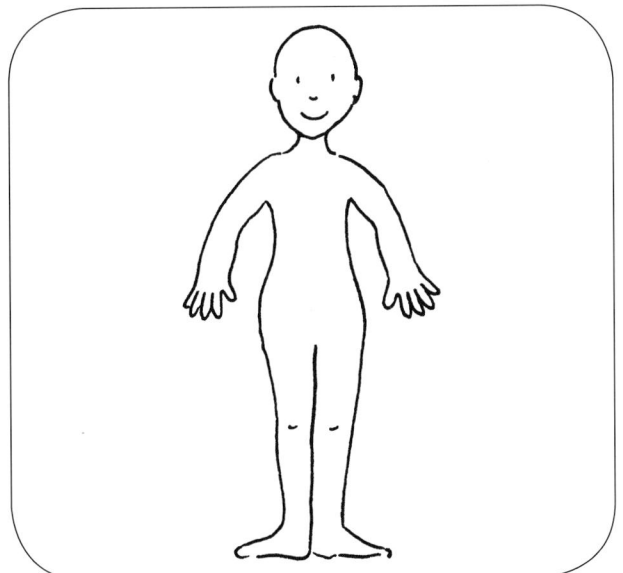 : "He (she) is wearing a … (blue shirt/red dress …)."

Listen and draw the clothes.

3. Take turns.

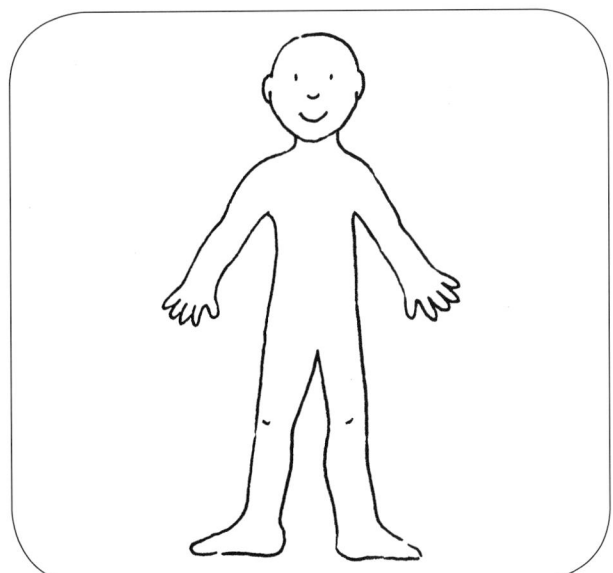

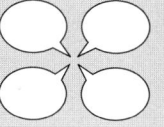
1. Work with partners

2. Hand out all the cards to the players

3.  : "Have you got … (the jeans, the shorts …)?"

   "Yes, I have. (Here you are.)"/"No, I haven't."

4. Take turns.

Have you got the shirt?

Yes, I have. Here you are.

Heike Jauernig/Jasmin Boller: Englisch an Stationen (Klasse 3)
© Auer Verlag

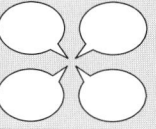

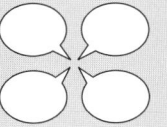
Heike Jauernig/Jasmin Boller: Englisch an Stationen (Klasse 3)
© Auer Verlag

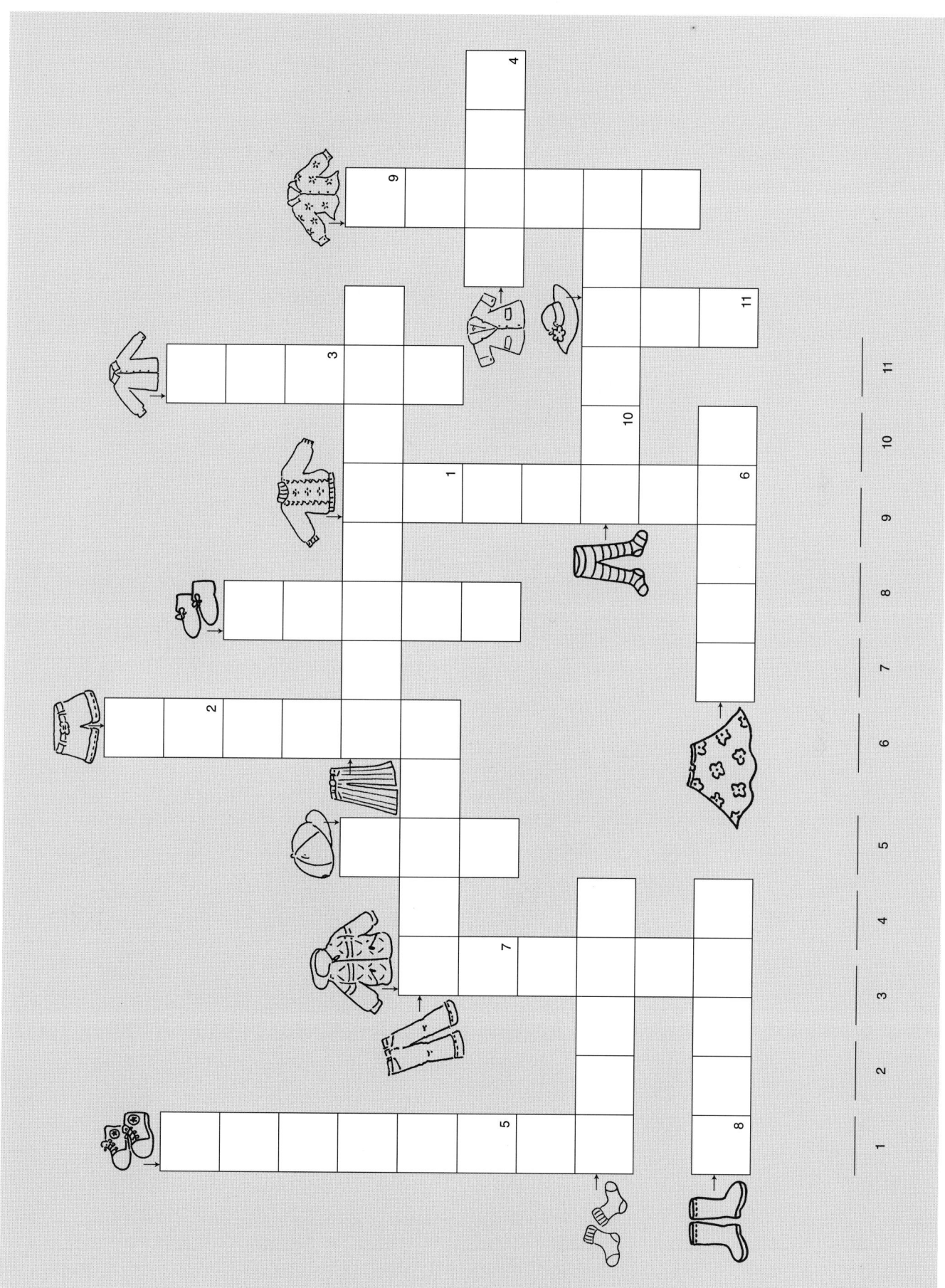

Fill in ____ ✎.

skirt trousers boots trainers shirt sweater hat cap tights shirt sweater hat cap tights socks jacket

1. Work with a partner  .

2. Mime a hobby (singing, reading, dancing …).

 : "Are you … (skiing, swimming …)?"

 : "Yes, I am."/"No, I am not."

3. Take turns and tick ✓ :

1. Fill in the missing letters ___✎.

2. Connect pictures with words.

p_la_ing   t_e   p_an_

_i_ing   a _i_e

d_nci_g

_lay_n_   _e_ _is

s_im_in_

_in_in_

r_a_ing

p_a_ing   _oot_ _ll

_ _ding   a   h_r_e

_ki_ng

a	a	b	b	d	d	e	f	g	g	g	g	h	i	i	i	k
l	m	n	n	n	o	o	p̸	p	r	r	s	s	s	t	w	y	y

Heike Jauernig/Jasmin Boller: Englisch an Stationen (Klasse 3)
© Auer Verlag

Yes, I do./No, I don't.

×   ✓

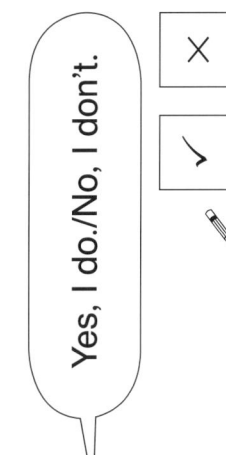

Do you like … (dancing, skiing …)?

name	dancing 	singing 	reading 	skiing	playing football	riding a bike	playing tennis	swimming	playing the piano	riding a horse					

Work with a partner  .

: "I like … (dancing …)." Listen and draw the hobby. Take turns and tick ✓:	: "I don't like … (singing …)." Listen and draw the hobby. Take turns and tick ✓:

 Present your work in class.

"… (Jenny) likes … (reading …)."
"… (Jenny) doesn't like … (skiing …)."

Heike Jauernig/Jasmin Boller: Englisch an Stationen (Klasse 3)
© Auer Verlag

Read  and fill in the name ____ .

Colin

Matt

Amy

Jillian

Kate

Bryan

She is wearing a skirt and likes dancing. She has got blonde hair.
Who is it?

It's _____

He is wearing trainers and likes playing football. He has got brown and curly hair.
Who is it?

It's _____

His hair is blonde. He is wearing shorts and a cap. He likes reading.
Who is it?

It's _____

Her hair is long. She is wearing a skirt and a pullover. She likes riding a bike.
Who is it?

It's _____

She likes dancing. She has got blonde hair and she is wearing a dress.
Who is it?

It's _____

His hair is blonde. He is wearing shorts and trainers. He likes playing football.
Who is it?

It's _____

Heike Jauernig/Jasmin Boller: Englisch an Stationen (Klasse 3)
© Auer Verlag

skiing   playing the piano   riding a horse   playing football

dancing   singing   swimming   riding a bike   playing tennis   reading

Heike Jauernig/Jasmin Boller: Englisch an Stationen (Klasse 3)
© Auer Verlag

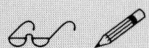
My friend

My friend's name is _____.

She/He has got _____ hair

and _____ eyes.

Her/His favourite pet is a _____

and h __ __ favourite colour is _____.

(Draw a picture of your friend.)

Today, she/he is wearing _____

_____.

(name) _____ 's telephone number is _____.

H__ __ favourite hobbies are _____

_____.

 Present your work in class!

Station 1 — Happy families

Food

1. Work with partners

2. Hand out all the cards to the players

3.  : "Have you got … (2 apples, 4 oranges …)?"

: "Yes, I have. (Here you are.)"
"No, I haven't."

Take turns.

Heike Jauernig/Jasmin Boller: Englisch an Stationen (Klasse 3)
© Auer Verlag

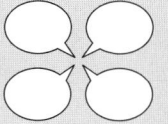
8	9	10

1

one peach

1	9	10

8

eight peaches

1	8	10

9

nine peaches

1	8	9

10

ten peaches

11	12	13

1

one pear

1	12	13

11

eleven pears

1	11	13

12

twelve pears

1	11	12

13

thirteen pears

13	14	15

1

one orange

1	14	15

13

thirteen oranges

1	13	15

14

fourteen oranges

1	13	14

15

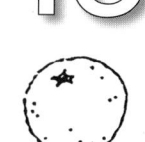

fifteen oranges

14	15	16

1

one cherry

1	15	16

14

fourteen cherries

1	14	16

15

fifteen cherries

1	14	15

16

sixteen cherries

Heike Jauernig/Jasmin Boller: Englisch an Stationen (Klasse 3)
© Auer Verlag

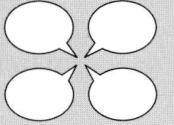

16	17	18

one strawberry

1	17	18

sixteen strawberries

1	16	18

seventeen strawberries

1	16	17

eighteen strawberries

18	19	20

one banana

1	19	20

eighteen bananas

1	18	20

nineteen bananas

1	18	19

twenty bananas

2	3	4

one apple

1	3	4

two apples

1	2	4

three apples

1	2	3

four apples

5	6	7

one lemon

1	6	7

five lemons

1	5	7

six lemons

1	5	6

seven lemons

Heike Jauernig/Jasmin Boller: Englisch an Stationen (Klasse 3)
© Auer Verlag

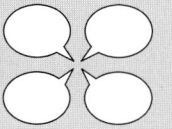
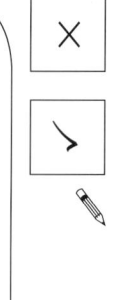

Yes, I do./No, I don't.

X
✓

Do you like ... (bananas, peaches ...)?

name	apples 	oranges 	strawberries 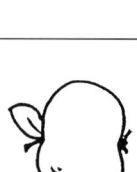	cherries 	lemons 	bananas	pears	peaches	

Heike Jauernig/Jasmin Boller: Englisch an Stationen (Klasse 3)
© Auer Verlag

1. Colour ✏ the fruit.

2. Work with a partner  .

 : "My … (pear, cherry …) is … (green, red, yellow …).
What colour is your …?"

 : "My … (pear, cherry …) is …
What colour is your … ?"

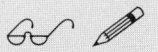
i	x	o	r	v	l	e	z	n	z	w	h	t	w	g
t	t	i	g	d	y	t	u	u	t	p	i	e	l	x
o	f	o	k	e	j	t	w	x	b	c	v	b	p	m
q	e	m	x	w	d	l	b	h	w	s	k	j	q	j
t	v	h	h	t	e	z	m	q	d	t	d	k	d	m
i	j	y	g	t	v	x	x	n	q	r	l	h	w	m
u	c	z	t	x	k	c	c	o	r	a	n	g	e	x
z	g	l	k	z	n	g	d	z	f	w	z	m	t	h
y	q	e	i	k	q	t	u	p	u	b	h	t	c	l
w	r	r	d	b	a	n	a	n	a	e	g	o	h	p
x	m	g	q	u	z	e	m	b	l	r	k	g	e	f
a	p	p	l	e	w	z	p	f	e	r	l	t	r	m
e	p	m	o	b	i	y	g	m	m	y	e	e	r	i
p	e	a	c	h	b	f	u	r	o	r	c	x	y	m
b	p	e	a	r	y	q	q	o	n	m	l	w	p	n

apple

banana

pear

peach

straw-
berry

lemon

cherry

orange

Colour the word and the picture in the same colour.

yellow

orange

blue

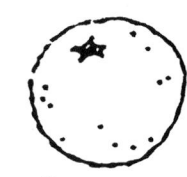
red

pink

purple

grey

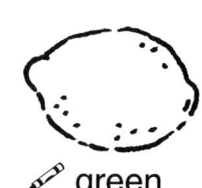
green

1. Work with a partner  .

2. Cut out ✂ and put the cards on the table.

: "Can I have some … (bread, butter …), please?"

: "Here you are."

: "Thank you."

: "You're welcome."

butter	bread	eggs
milk	cheese	jam
honey	toast	hot chocolate

58

Heike Jauernig/Jasmin Boller: Englisch an Stationen (Klasse 3)
© Auer Verlag

butter   milk   cheese   jam

honey   hot chocolate   eggs   toast   bread

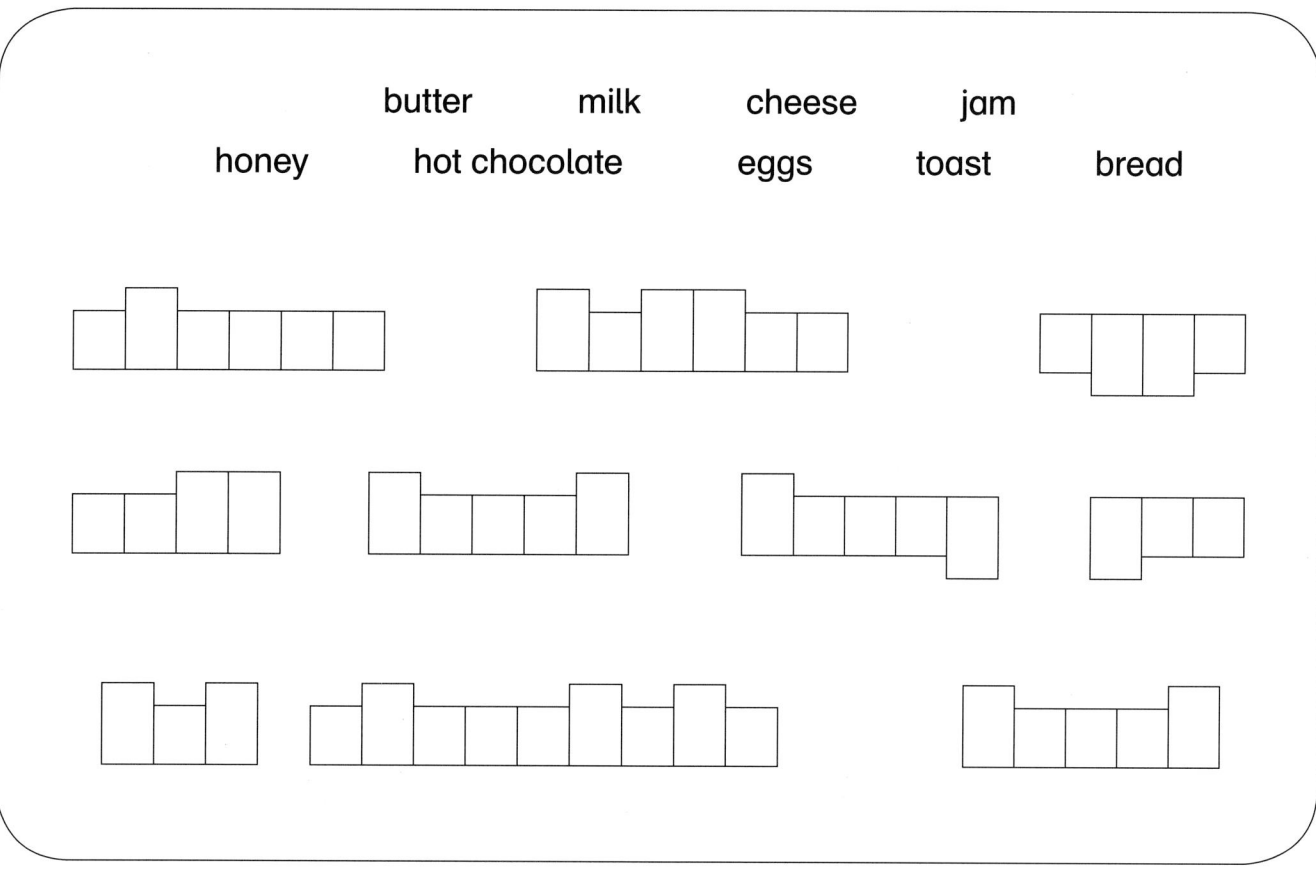

Heike Jauernig/Jasmin Boller: Englisch an Stationen (Klasse 3)
© Auer Verlag

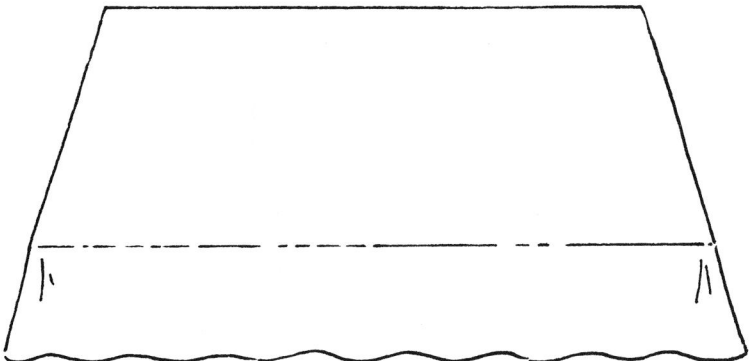
Read and draw ✐.

Kate likes toast, jam and eggs for breakfast.

Colin likes bread, honey and milk for breakfast.

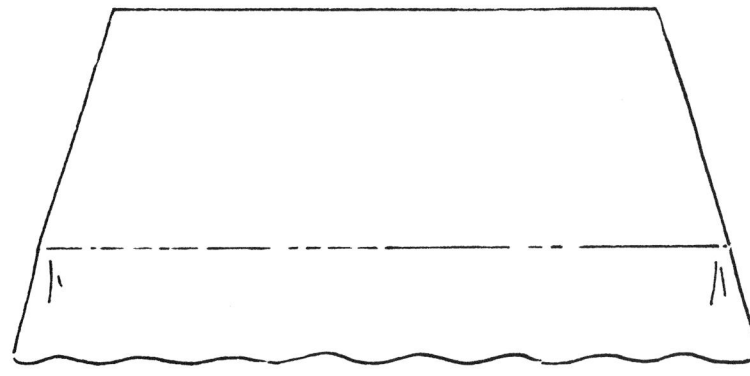

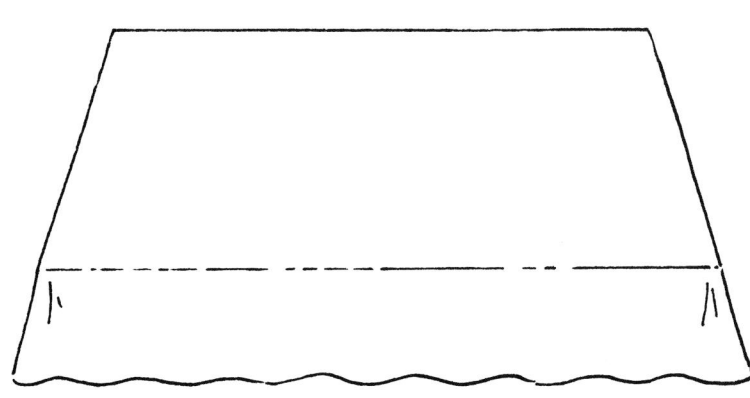

Amy likes toast, butter, cheese and hot chocolate for breakfast.

Heike Jauernig/Jasmin Boller: Englisch an Stationen (Klasse 3)
© Auer Verlag

 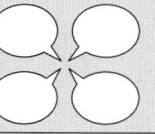

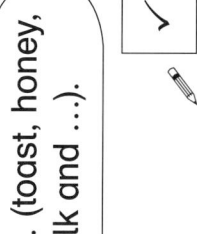

I like ... (toast, honey, milk and ...).

What do you like for breakfast?

name	toast	bread	butter	honey	jam	cheese	eggs	milk	hot chocolate

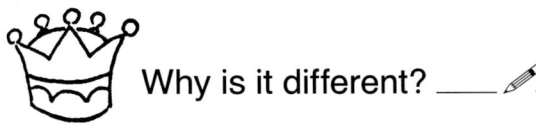
Cross the odd one out ✗ 🖊.

Why is it different? ____ 🖊.

1.	butter	toast	cat	jam	_____
2.	honey	trainers	cheese	bread	_____
3.	jam	eggs	singing	hot chocolate	_____
4.	football	milk	toast	honey	_____
5.	bread	jam	shorts	milk	_____
6.	cheese	turtle	eggs	hot chocolate	_____
7.	milk	butter	cheese	stocking	_____

Heike Jauernig/Jasmin Boller: Englisch an Stationen (Klasse 3)
© Auer Verlag

Station 10 Unscramble letters! — Food

1. Unscramble the letters and write ___ the words.

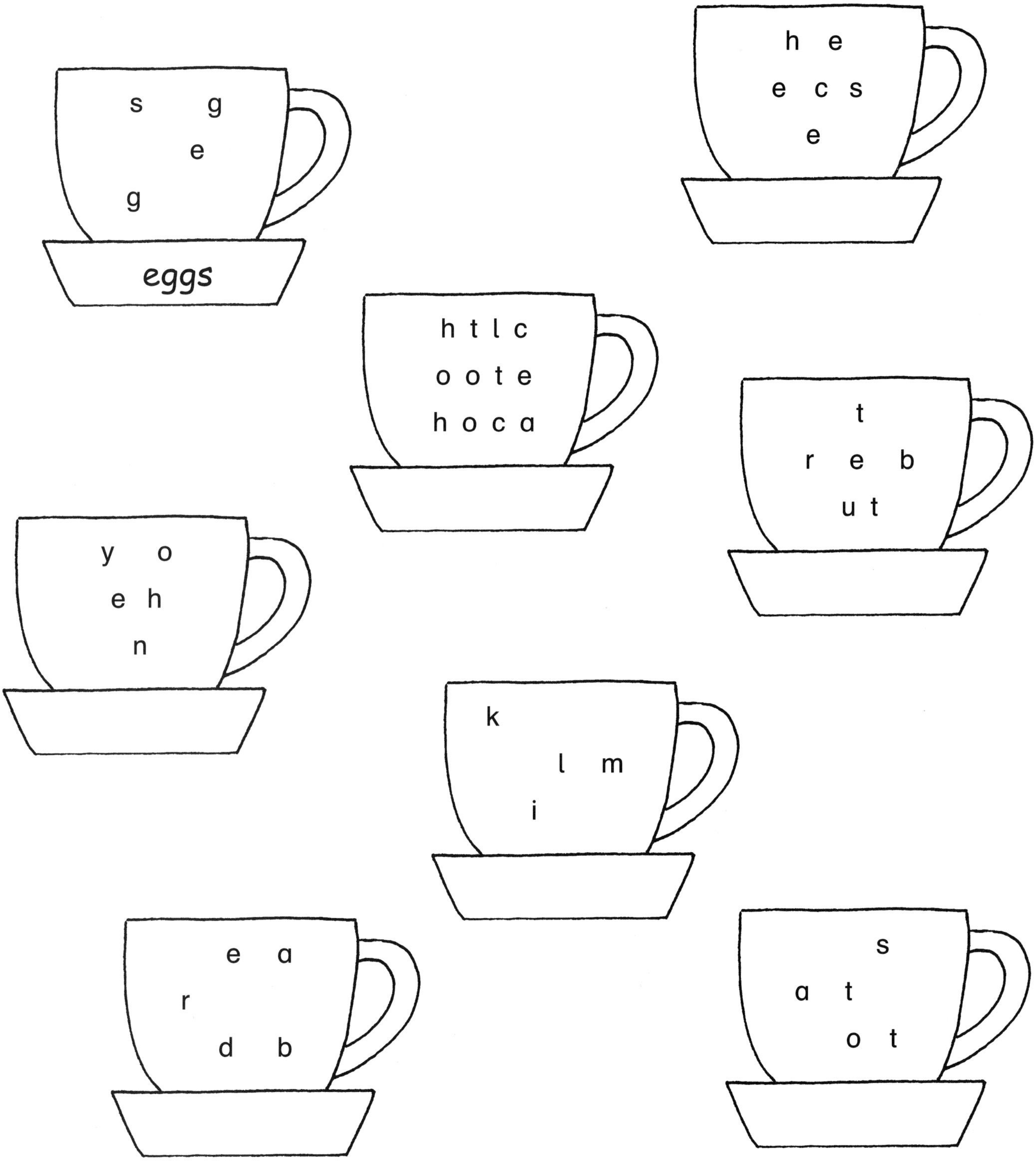
s g e g
eggs
h e e c s e
h t l c o o t e h o c a
t r e b u t
y o e h n
k l m i
e a r d b
s a t o t

2. Which word is missing? ______________________

eggs, hot chocolate, jam, cheese, butter, honey, milk, bread, toast

What's on the sandwich? Write ____ the words.

It's a sandwich with _____

_____

_____

_____

_____

_____

_____

_____

_____

eggs, lettuce, cheese, cucumbers,
ham, salami, tomatoes

Heike Jouernig/Jasmin Boller: Englisch an Stationen (Klasse 3)
© Auer Verlag

Station 12 Cross word puzzle

Food

tomatoes, toast, cucumbers, butter, cheese, ham, eggs, lettuce, salami

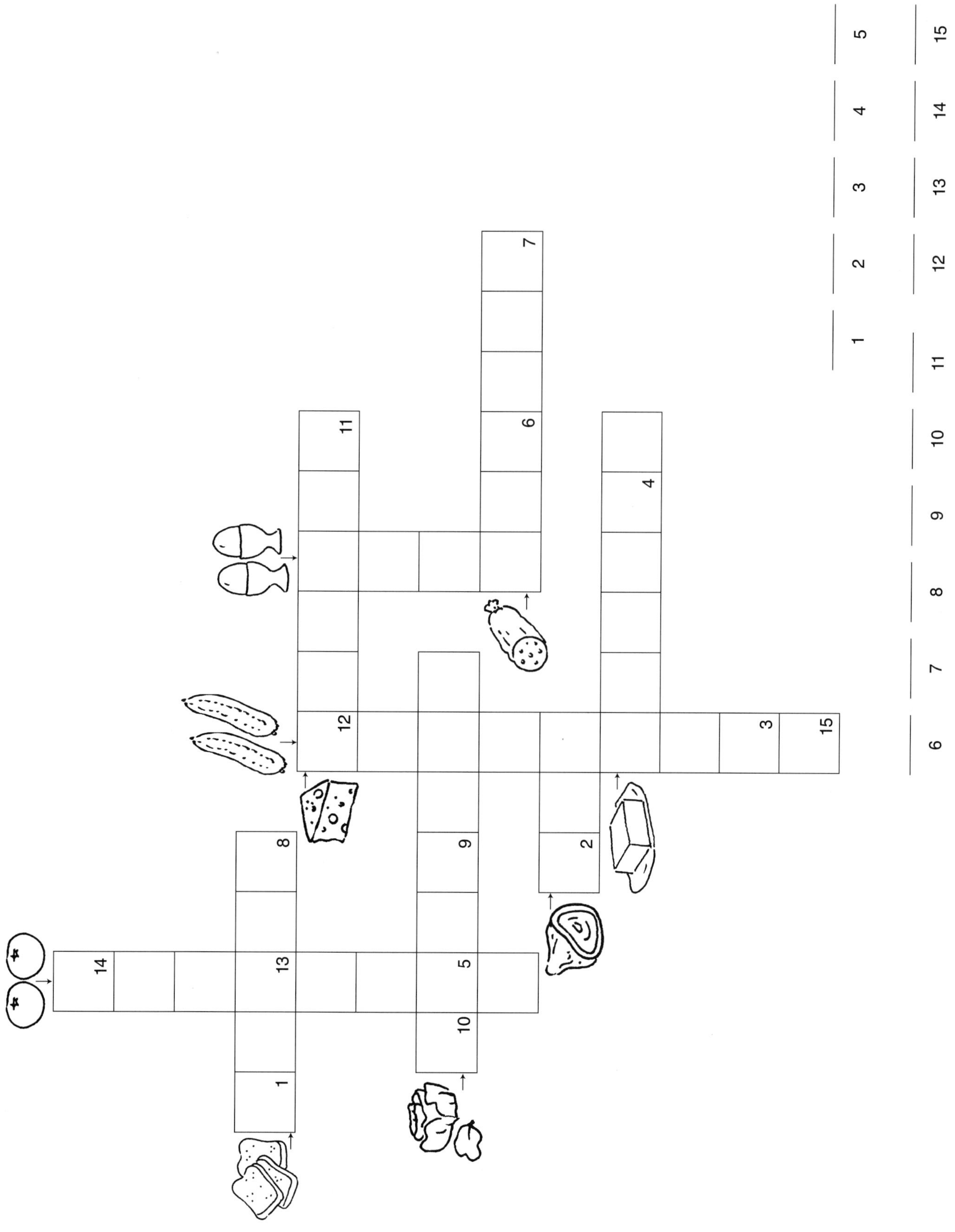

Fill in the missing letters ___ .

Colin has got a s _a_ n ___ wich with b ___ ead, s ___ l ___ m ___ ,
___ ucu ___ be ___ s and ___ ___ ttuce.

Jillian has got a sandwi ___ ___ with t ___ as ___ , h ___ m,
t ___ m ___ t ___ es and e ___ g ___ .

Matt has got a sandw ___ ch with brea ___ and ___ oa ___ t,
chee ___ e, ___ utte ___ and le ___ tu ___ e.

Amy has got a ___ andwich with ___ read, bu ___ ___ er,
___ oma ___ oes, ___ u ___ umb ___ rs and ___ ett ___ ce.

ȧ	a	a	a	a	b	b	c	c	c	c	c	d	d	e	e
g	h	i	i	l	l	m	o	o	o	r	r	r			
s	s	s	s	t	t	t	t	t	t	t	u				

Heike Jauernig/Jasmin Boller: Englisch an Stationen (Klasse 3)
© Auer Verlag

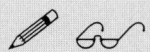
Cross the odd one out ✕ ✐. 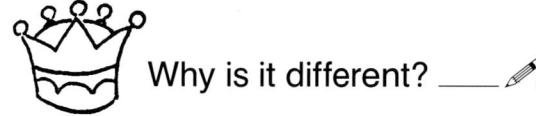 Why is it different? ____ ✐.

1. tomatoes   toast   cucumbers   seven   _____

2. hat   ham   cheese   butter   _____

3. lettuce   eggs   singing   salami   _____

4. cucumbers   sweater   toast   ham   _____

5. cat   butter   lettuce   cheese   _____

6. cheese   toast   eggs   present   _____

7. blue   cucumbers   tomatoes   salami   _____

8. salami   ham   bread   shoe   _____

9. eggs   dancing   butter   lettuce   _____

10. ham   tomatoes   cucumbers   turtle   _____

1. Unscramble the letters and write ___ ✏ the words.

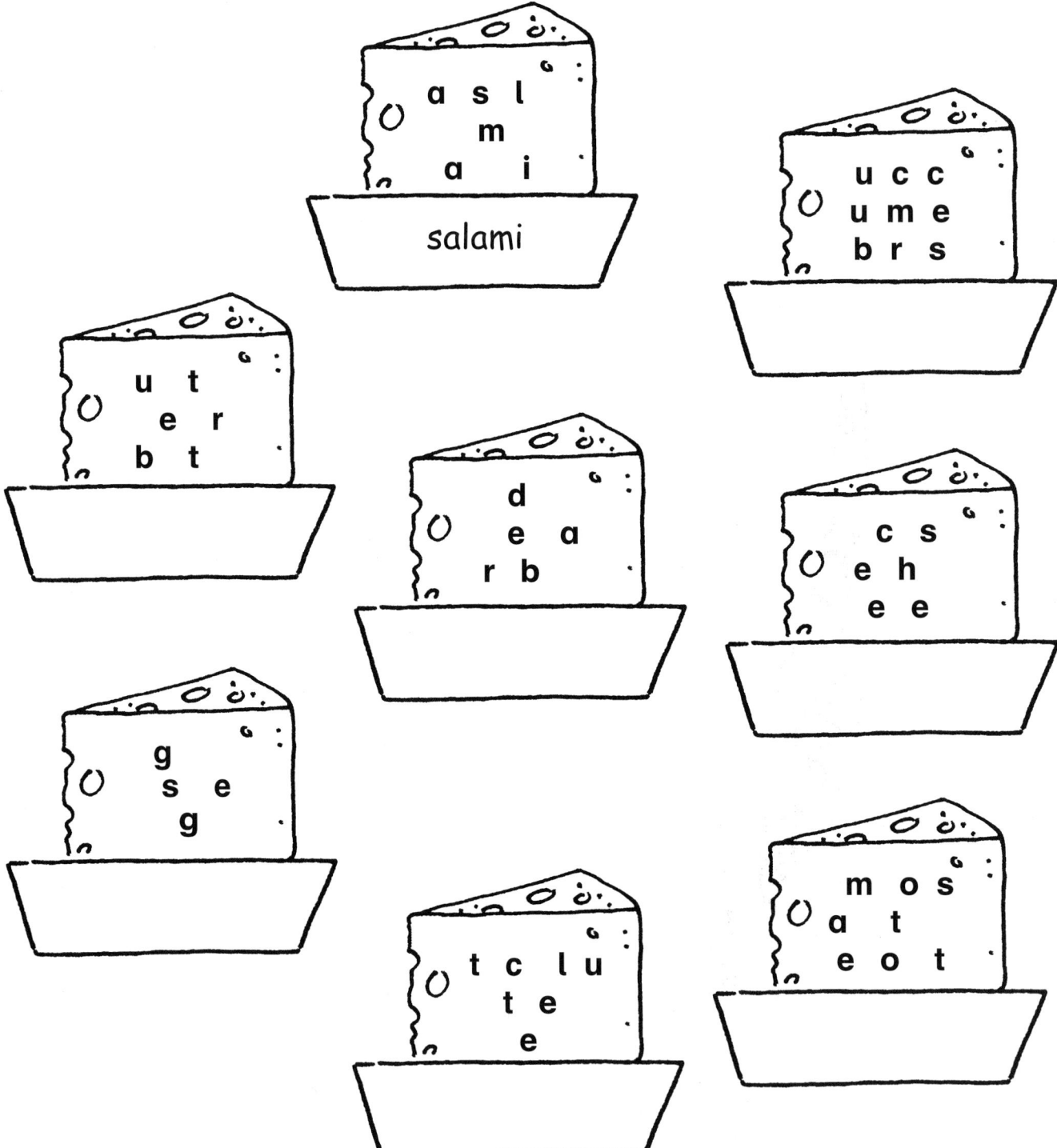

salami

2. Which word is missing? _____

| tomatoes, salami, cheese, ham, cucumbers, lettuce, butter, eggs, bread |

Heike Jouernig/Jasmin Boller: Englisch an Stationen (Klasse 3)
© Auer Verlag

Laufzettel

für _____

PFLICHTSTATIONEN

Stationsnummer	Erledigt am	Kontrolliert am
Nummer _____		
Nummer _____		
Nummer _____		
Nummer _____		
Nummer _____		
Nummer _____		
Nummer _____		
Nummer _____		

WAHLSTATIONEN

Stationsnummer	Erledigt am	Kontrolliert am
Nummer _____		
Nummer _____		
Nummer _____		
Nummer _____		
Nummer _____		
Nummer _____		
Nummer _____		

Lösungen

Christmas/Station 2 Seite 21

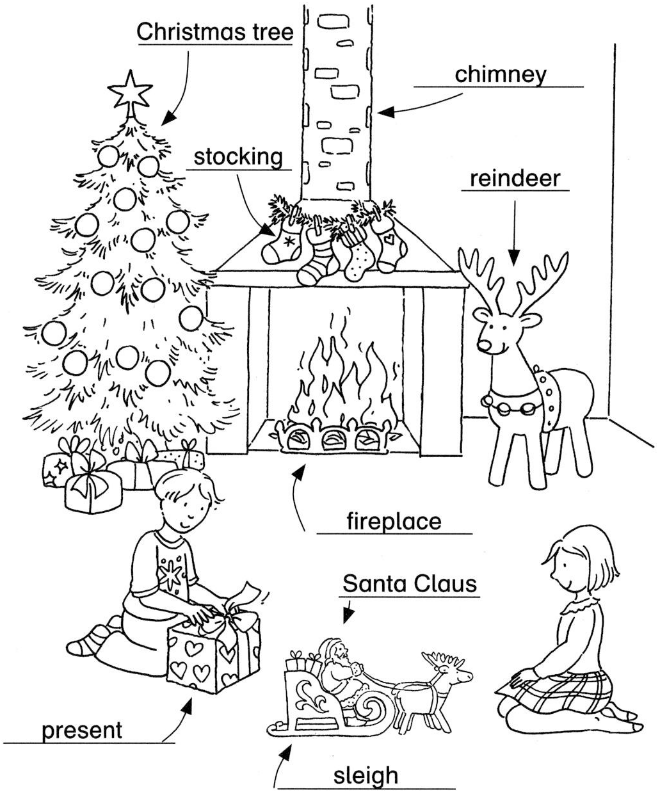
Christmas tree
chimney
stocking
reindeer
fireplace
Santa Claus
present
sleigh

Christmas/Station 3 Seite 22

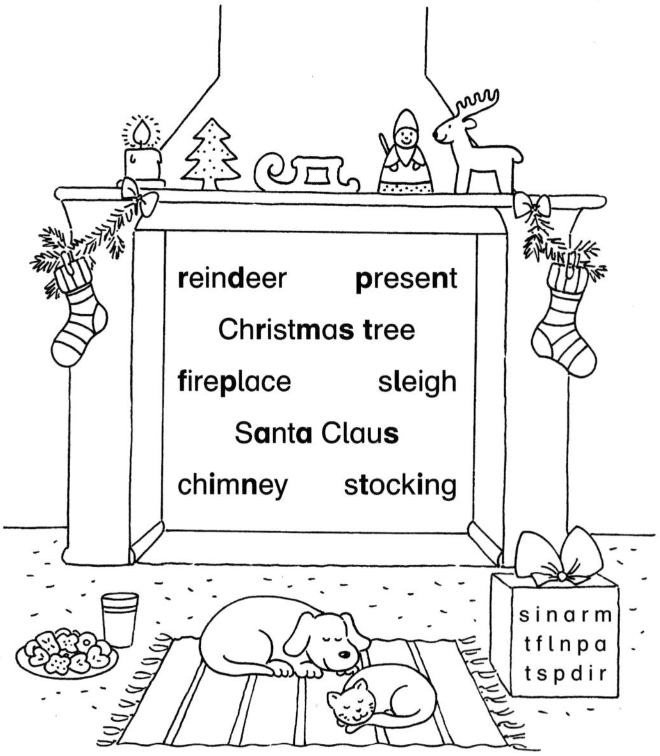
reindeer present
Christmas tree
fireplace sleigh
Santa Claus
chimney stocking
s i n a r m
t f l n p a
t s p d i r

Christmas/Station 4 — Seite 23

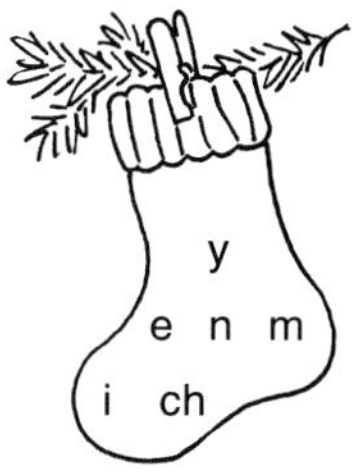
y
e n m
i ch

chimney

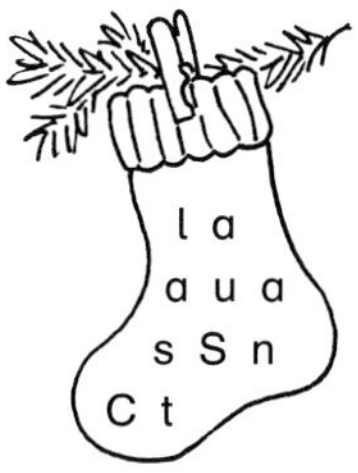
l a
a u a
s S n
C t

Santa Claus

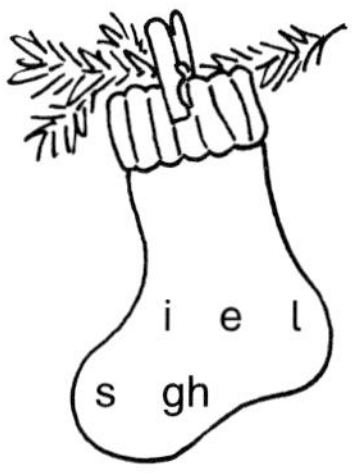
i e l
s gh

sleigh

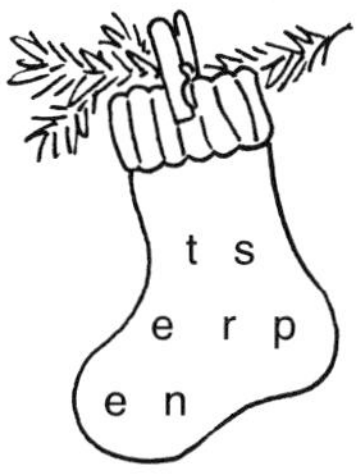
t s
e r p
e n

present

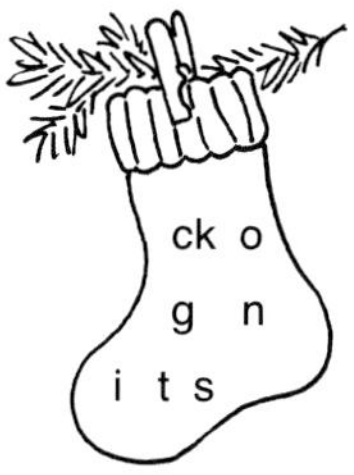
ck o
g n
i t s

stocking

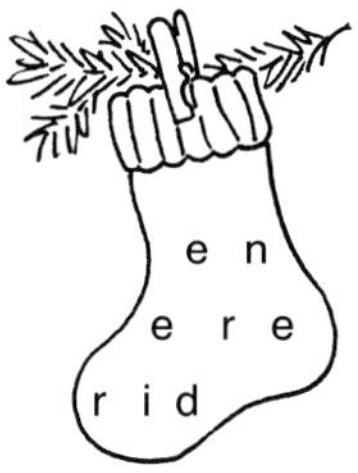
e n
e r e
r i d

reindeer

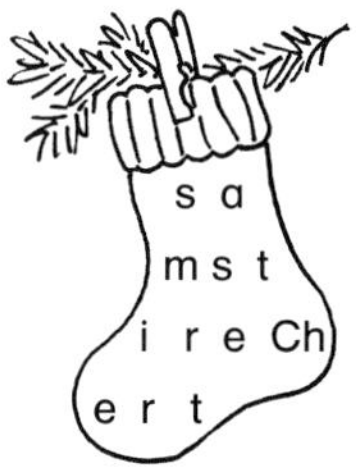
s a
m s t
i r e Ch
e r t

Christmas tree

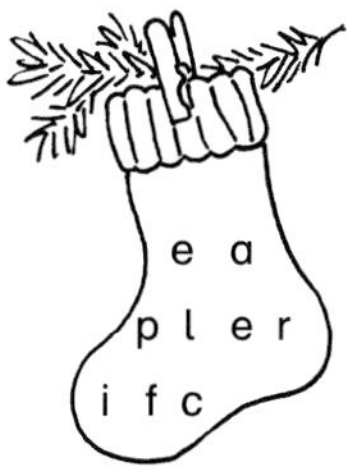
e a
p l e r
i f c

fireplace

Christmas/Station 6 — Seite 25

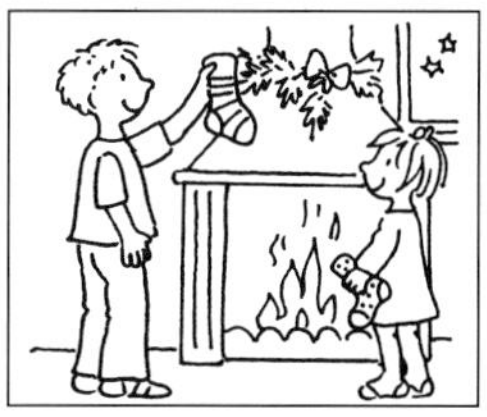

The children put stockings on the fire-place on Christmas Eve.

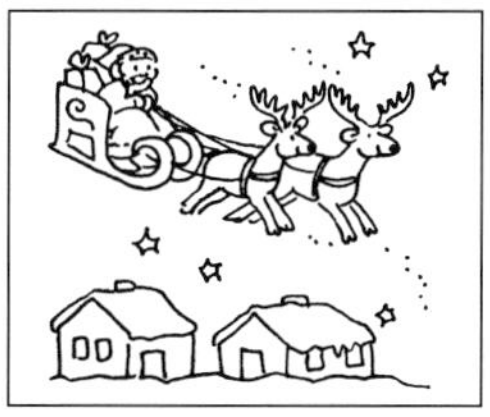

Santa Claus comes at night.

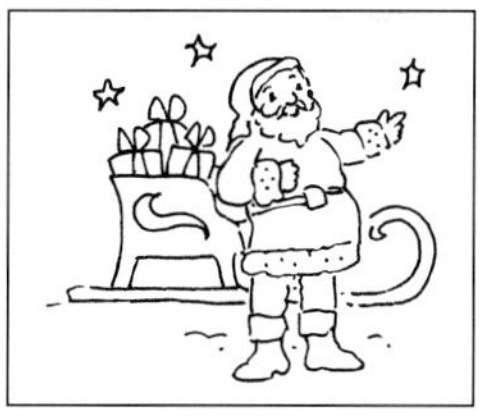

He has got a sleigh.

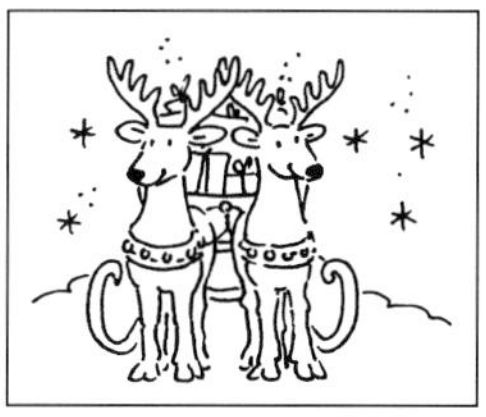

The reindeer pull the sleigh.

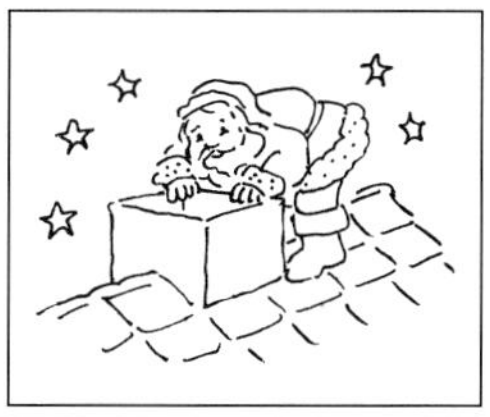

Santa Claus comes down the chimney.

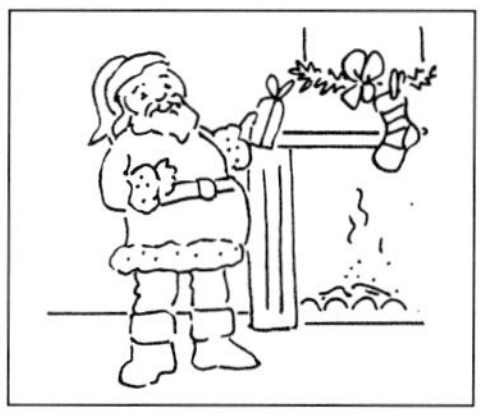

He puts the presents into the stockings.

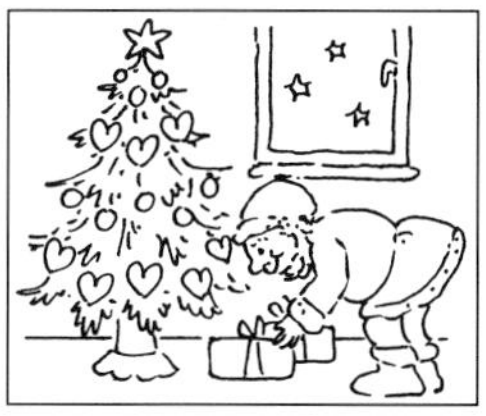

He puts the big presents under the Christmas tree.

On December 25 in the morning, the children look inside the stockings.

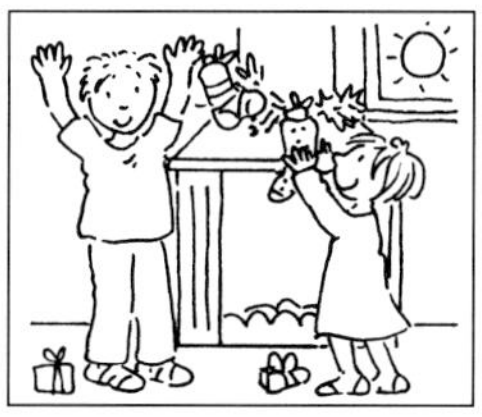

This is a fish. It can swim.

This is a guinea pig. Its colour is brown.

Amy has got a cat. It is six years old.

This is a rat. It can run.

This is Bryan's budgie. It has got two eyes.

Jillian has got a dog. Its colour is black.

This is Matt's turtle. It has got four legs.

Kate has got a rabbit. Its colour is white.

C	V	Z	X	C	M	T	B	U	D	G	I	E	R	N
F	B	T	Y	P	E	L	J	X	Y	O	D	A	T	N
A	K	I	U	C	S	T	U	R	T	L	E	Z	U	F
M	J	D	T	P	H	K	W	P	K	G	Q	R	G	T
N	R	X	U	I	D	Y	T	W	Q	S	L	A	I	U
X	R	K	Z	M	J	G	X	C	S	H	V	T	S	C
T	A	Q	L	A	M	R	J	C	Q	J	I	D	O	G
W	B	X	O	F	D	J	F	A	O	Z	P	A	H	K
F	B	U	G	P	R	M	E	T	L	D	F	A	T	V
Q	I	J	G	U	I	N	E	A	X	P	I	G	E	H
X	T	M	D	J	Z	G	H	W	K	O	S	F	X	E
P	R	Z	A	W	Z	V	K	I	H	N	H	X	U	S
Q	E	S	F	Y	G	A	B	R	P	G	B	Y	I	X
E	R	R	M	F	G	V	Y	M	O	B	Q	F	M	U
I	I	A	Z	U	O	N	N	W	Z	O	N	C	Z	Z

These pets can run:

These pets have got four legs:

These pets cannot climb:

These pets have got ears:

These pets cannot fly:

1. t-shirt	blouse	~~nine~~	shorts	number
2. trainers	~~budgie~~	boots	shoes	pet/animal
3. ~~hair~~	jeans	pullover	shorts	bodypart
4. jacket	coat	~~green~~	blouse	colour
5. skirt	~~seven~~	shirt	trousers	number
6. tights	dress	skirt	~~dog~~	pet/animal
7. ~~turtle~~	socks	cap	hat	pet/animal
8. sweater	trainers	coat	~~purple~~	colour
9. ~~foot~~	shirt	jacket	shoes	bodypart
10. t-shirt	~~white~~	tights	jeans	colour

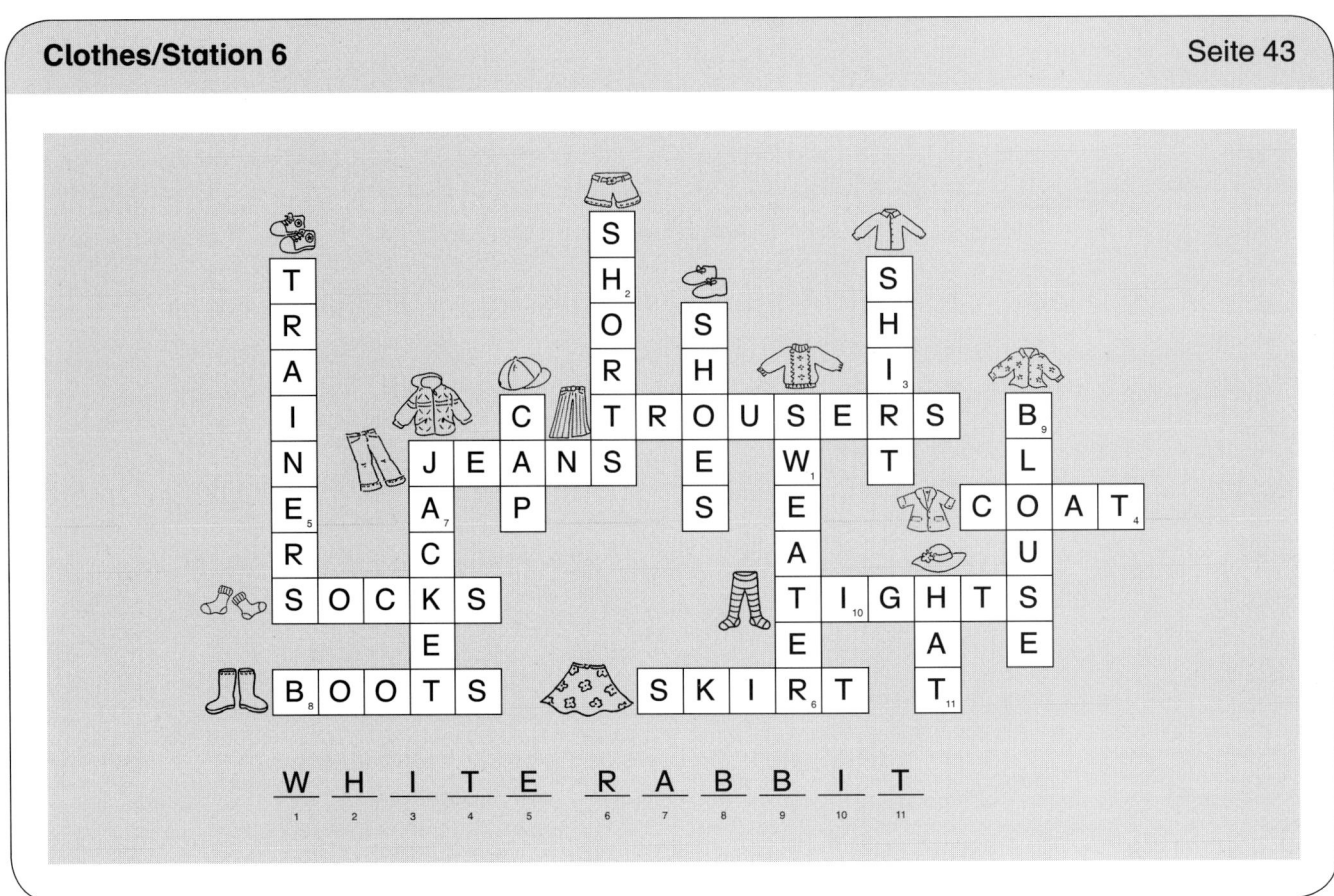

Clothes/Station 6

Seite 43

TRAINERS
SHORTS
SHOES
SHIRT
CAP
TROUSERS
BLOUSE
JEANS
JACKET
COAT
SWEATER
SOCKS
TIGHTS
HAT
BOOTS
SKIRT
W H I T E R A B B I T
1 2 3 4 5 6 7 8 9 10 11

Clothes/Station 7

Seite 44

hat
sweater
cap
skirt
tights
jacket
shirt
boots
socks
trousers
trainers

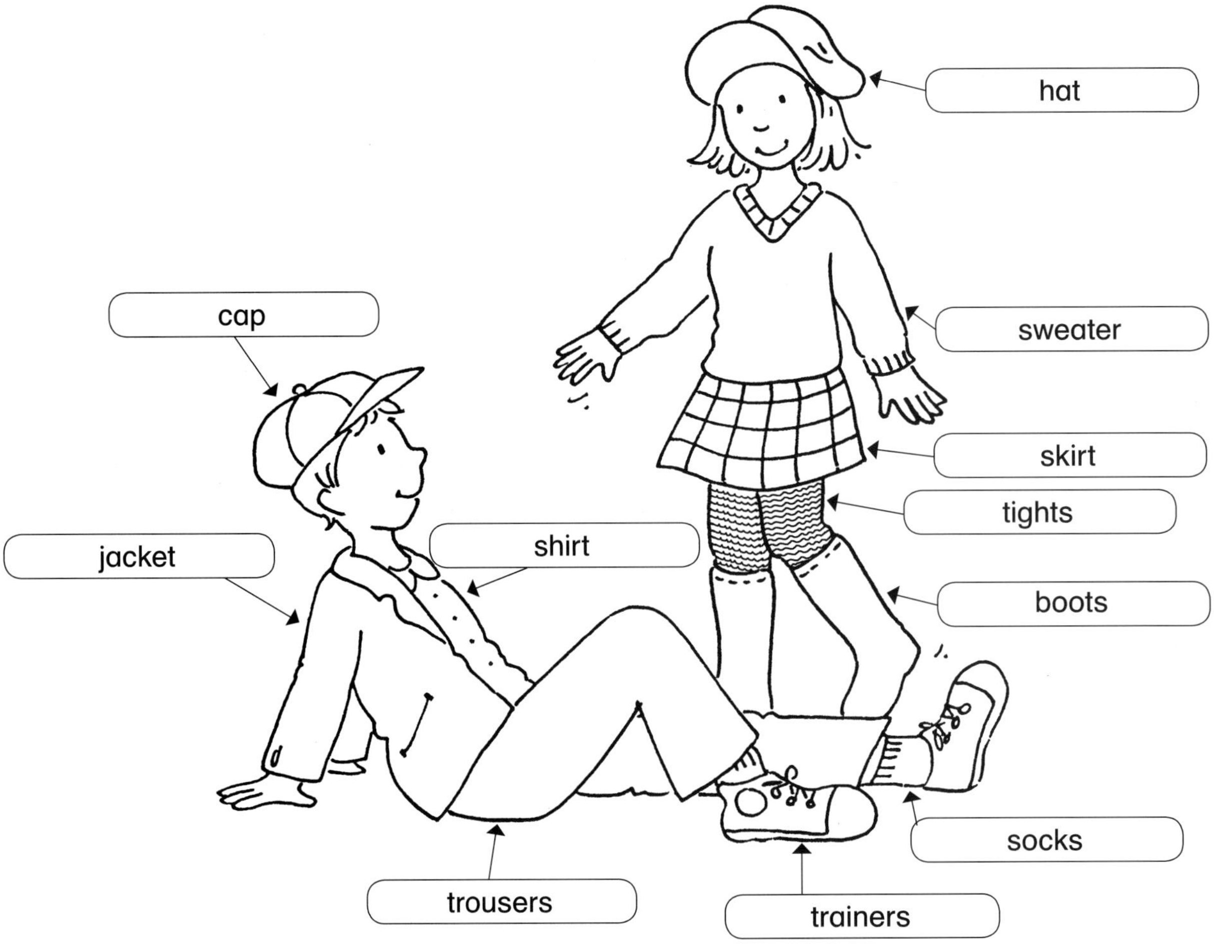

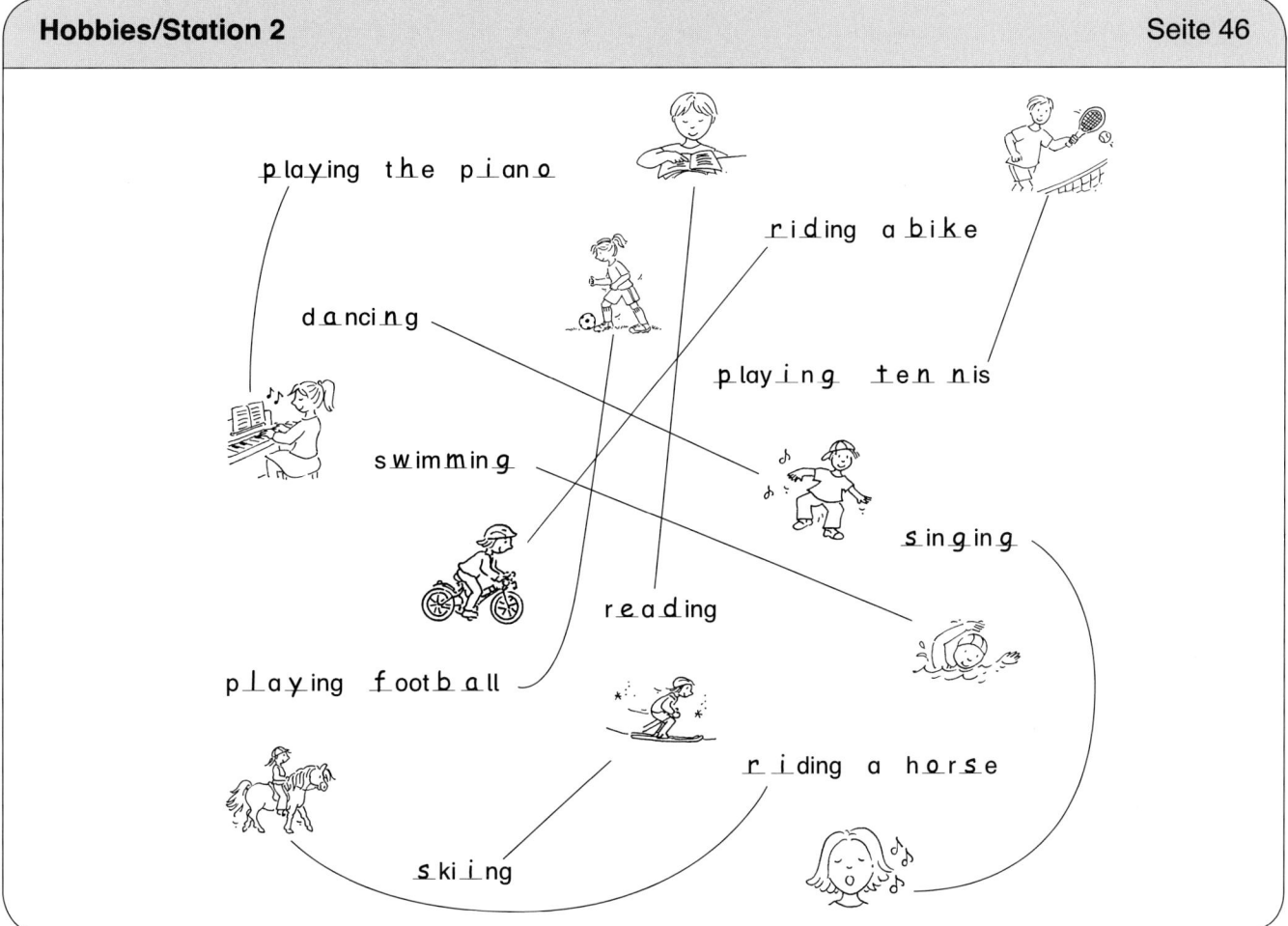

playing the piano

dancing

riding a bike

playing tennis

swimming

singing

reading

playing football

riding a horse

skiing

His hair is blonde. He is wearing shorts and trainers. He likes playing football. Who is it?
It's Colin.

Her hair is long. She is wearing a skirt and a pullover. She likes riding a bike. Who is it?
It's Kate.

He is wearing trainers and likes playing football. He has got brown and curly hair. Who is it?
It's Matt.

She likes dancing. She has got blonde hair and she is wearing a dress. Who is it?
It's Amy.

His hair is blonde. He is wearing shorts and a cap. He likes reading. Who is it?
It's Bryan.

She is wearing a skirt and likes dancing. She has got blonde hair. Who is it?
It's Jillian.

| playing tennis |

| skiing |

| playing football |

| singing |

| playing the piano |

| reading |

| riding a horse |

| dancing |

| swimming |

| riding a bike |

i	x	o	r	v	l	e	z	n	z	w	h	t	w	g
t	t	i	g	d	y	t	u	u	t	p	i	e	l	x
o	f	o	k	e	j	t	w	x	b	c	v	b	p	m
q	e	m	x	w	d	l	b	h	w	s	k	j	q	j
t	v	h	h	t	e	z	m	q	d	t	d	k	d	m
i	j	y	g	t	v	x	x	n	q	r	l	h	w	m
u	c	z	t	x	k	c	c	o	r	a	n	g	e	x
z	g	l	k	z	n	g	d	z	f	w	z	m	t	h
y	q	e	i	k	q	t	u	p	u	b	h	t	c	l
w	r	r	d	b	a	n	a	n	a	e	g	o	h	p
x	m	g	q	u	z	e	m	b	l	r	k	g	e	f
a	p	p	l	e	w	z	p	f	e	r	l	t	r	m
e	p	m	o	b	i	y	g	m	m	y	e	e	r	i
p	e	a	c	h	b	f	u	r	o	r	c	x	y	m
b	p	e	a	r	y	q	q	o	n	m	l	w	p	n

Food/Station 6 — Seite 59

cheese   butter   eggs

milk   toast   honey   jam

hot chocolate   bread

Food/Station 9 — Seite 62

1. butter   toast   ~~cat~~   jam   pet/animal
2. honey   ~~trainers~~ cheese   bread   clothes
3. jam   eggs   ~~singing~~   hot chocolate   hobby
4. ~~football~~ milk   toast   honey   hobby
5. bread   jam   ~~shorts~~   milk   clothes
6. cheese   ~~turtle~~   eggs   hot chocolate   pet/animal
7. milk   butter   cheese   ~~stocking~~   Christmas

Food/Station 10 — Seite 63

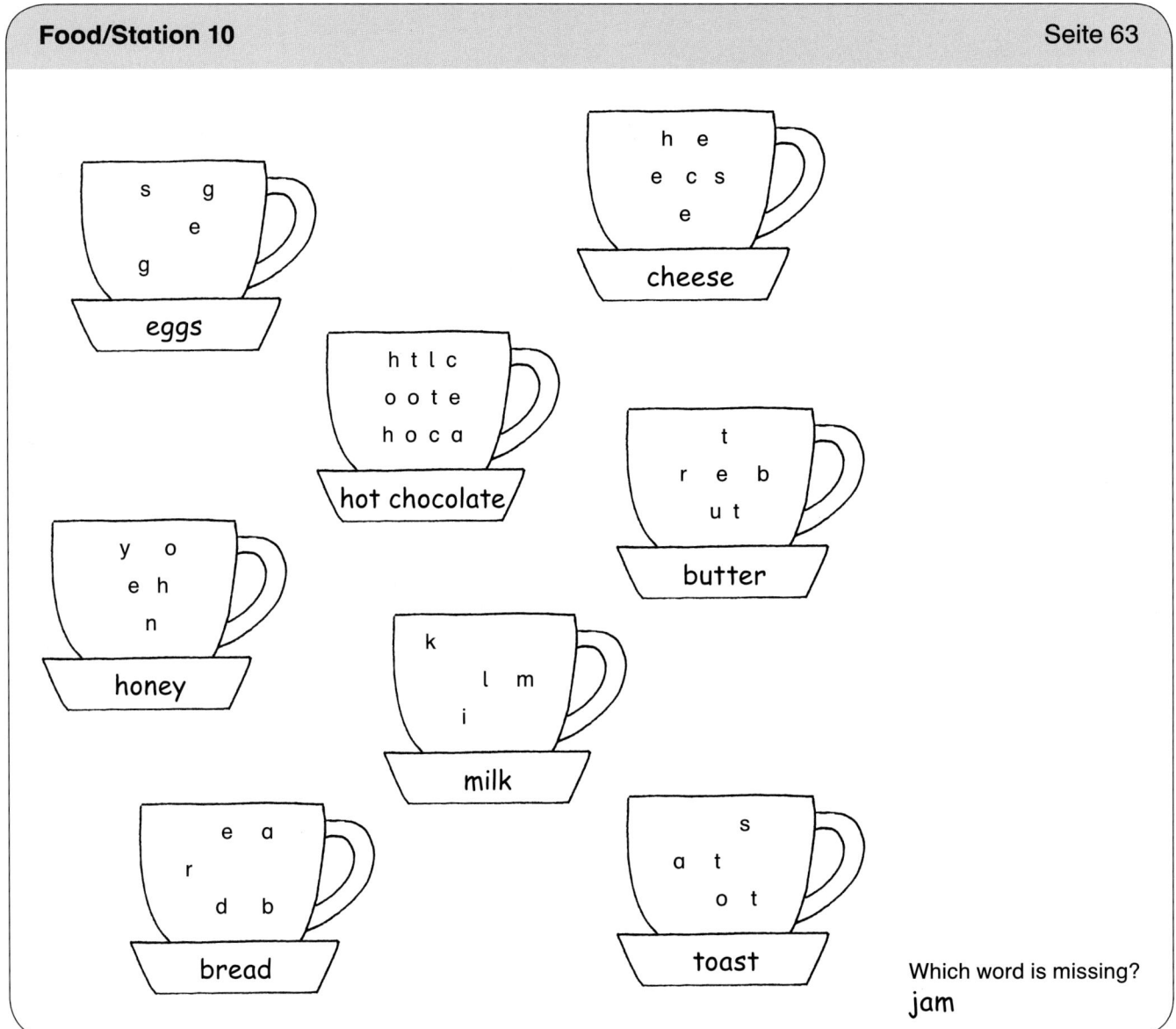

Which word is missing?
jam

78

It's a sandwich with lettuce, tomatoes, salami and cucumbers.

It's a sandwich with tomatoes, cheese and cucumbers.

It's a sandwich with eggs, tomatoes and lettuce.

It's a sandwich with ham, cucumbers, cheese and lettuce.

T₁₄ O M A S T₈
T O A₁₃ S T₈
C₁₂ H E E S E₁₁
T E G
L₁₀ E₅ T T₉ U C E G
S S A L₆ A M I₇
H₂ A M B
B U T T E₄ R
E
R₃
S₁₅

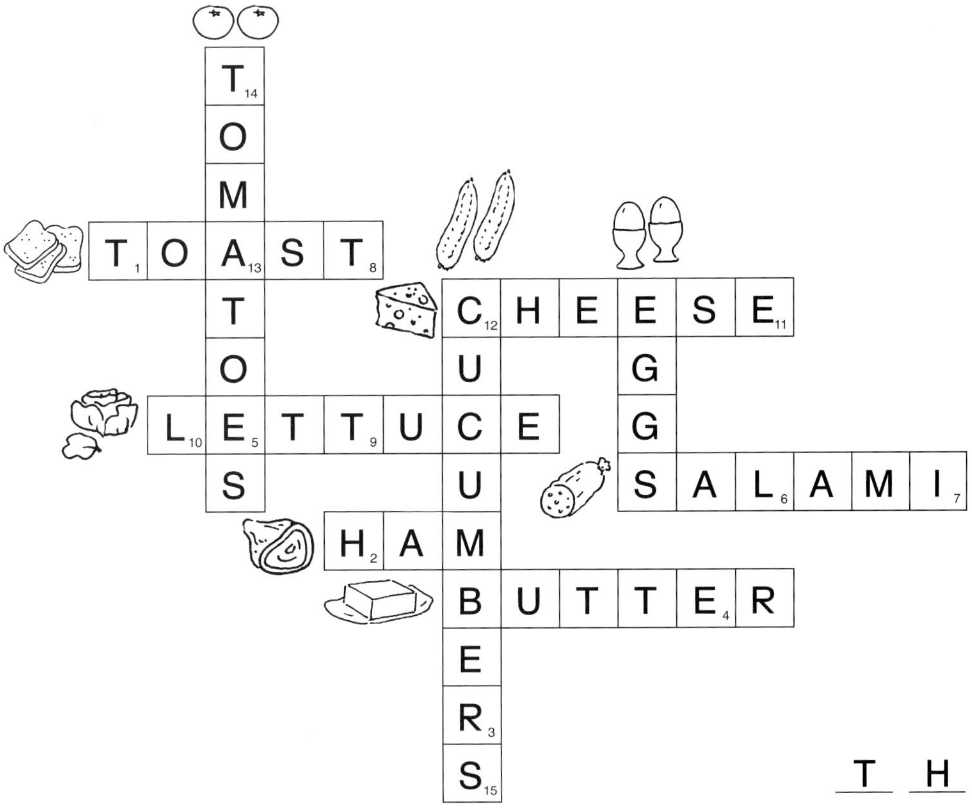

T H R E E
1 2 3 4 5

L I T T L E C A T S
6 7 8 9 10 11 12 13 14 15

79

Food/Station 13

Colin has got a **sand**wich with **b**read, **s**al**a**mi, **c**ucu**mb**ers and **le**ttuce.

Jillian has got a sandwi**ch** with **to**a**st**, h**a**m, **to**m**at**oes and e**gg**s.

Matt has got a sandwi**c**h with brea**d** and **toas**t, chee**s**e, **butt**er and lettu**c**e.

Amy has got a **s**andwich with **b**read, bu**tt**er, **t**oma**t**oes, **c**ucumb**e**rs and le**ttuc**e.

Food/Station 14

1. tomatoes	toast	cucumbers	~~seven~~	number
2. ~~hat~~	ham	cheese	butter	clothes
3. lettuce	eggs	~~singing~~	salami	hobby
4. cucumbers	~~sweater~~	toast	ham	clothes
5. ~~cat~~	butter	lettuce	cheese	pet/animal
6. cheese	toast	eggs	~~present~~	christmas
7. ~~blue~~	cucumbers	tomatoes	salami	colour
8. salami	ham	bread	~~shoe~~	clothes
9. eggs	~~dancing~~	butter	lettuce	hobby
10. ham	tomatoes	cucumbers	~~turtle~~	pet/animal

Food/Station 15

salami

cucumbers

butter

bread

cheese

eggs

lettuce

tomatoes

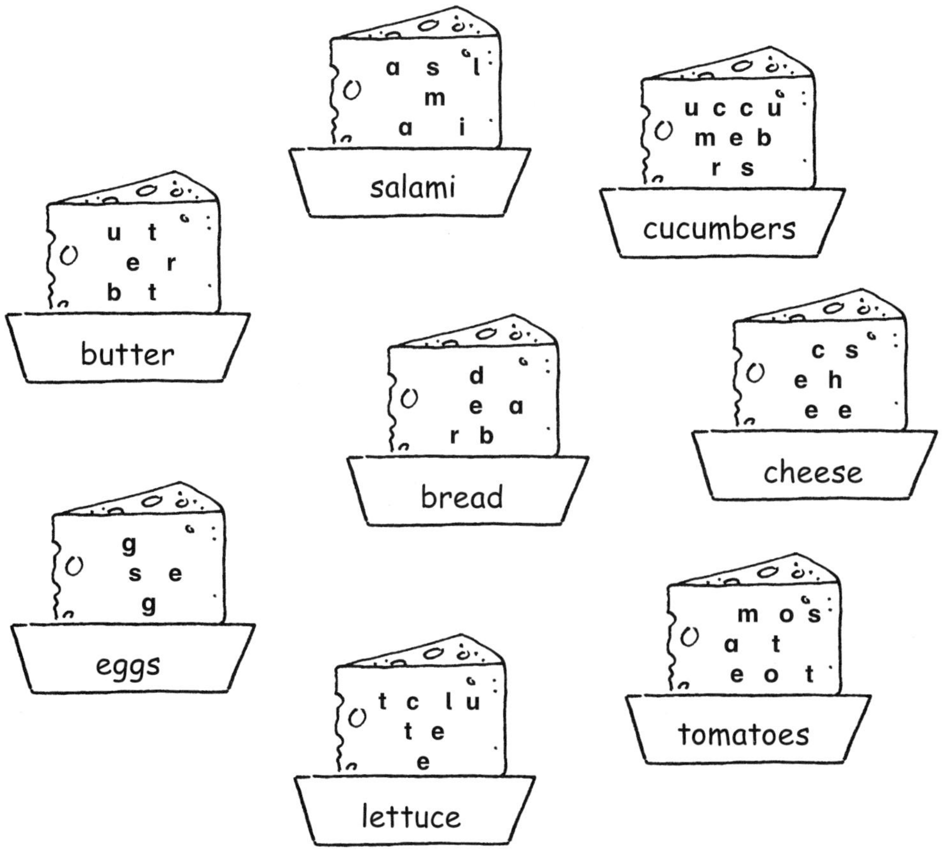

Which word is missing?

ham